M W
& R

BECOMING FEMINISTS

C L

Edited by Lynn Crosbie

I C K

B E C O M I N G

feminists

Macfarlane Walter & Ross

Toronto

Macfarlane Walter & Ross
37A Hazelton Avenue
Toronto, Canada M5R 2E3

Canadian Cataloguing in Publication Data

Main entry under title:

Click: becoming feminists

ISBN 1-55199-004-0

1. Feminism   2. Women - Social conditions.
I. Crosbie, Lynn, 1963-   .

HQ1206.C54 1997   305.42   C97-931916-1

Printed and bound in Canada

Macfarlane Walter & Ross gratefully acknowledges
the support of the Canada Council for the Arts and
the Ontario Arts Council for its publishing program.

For my mother, with love

C L I C K

ACK NOW LEDGMENTS

PARTICULARLY want to thank Sara Borins (who conceived of this book) for her hard work, inspiration, vision, and friendship.

I also want to thank Jan Walter and Paul Woods for their remarkable support, wisdom, and assistance.

Finally, I wish to thank the following people for their help, ideas, and interest:

Joanne Balles, Teresa Casas,
Mark Connery, Barbara Czarnecki,
Sky Gilbert, Malcolm Ingram,
Joe Matt,
Al McMullin,
Ira Silverberg,
Michael Turner,
R. M. Vaughan,

and, with much love,

Michael Holmes.

CLICK

CLICK Intro

Not to mention delight laughter feminism
upon which I keep insisting

   – Erin Mouré, "Human Bearing"

BRA ASHES

   – Inscribed on an urn on my mother's shelf, circa 1975

duction

L Y N N C R O S B I E

I N RECENT MONTHS I have heard hyper-masculine men, ranging from gangster rappers to uniformed members of the World Wrestling Federation, refer to themselves and their cronies as "cliques" (pronounced "clicks"). This particular choice of word, in my mind, recalls feminism's pluralistic nature and suggests that, finally, aggressive men have come to bite off feminism for fast and frightening images of strength.

It was Gloria Steinem who used the term *click* to describe that moment of feminist self-awareness, the quick epiphany that has a private and public resonance: the click of high heels on sidewalks or tapped together in a ruby glitter; two fingers snapping; scissor blades closing; the release of a gun's safety; the flick of a light switch; a catch in the machinery; the clatter of nails on a typewriter; a lock yielding to a key.

In the late 1960s, feminists made this sound every time they flicked open a lighter to torch a bra, or pounded the pavement in protest. When I began asking women to contribute to this collection, I wasn't sure if the term still had any currency. So I began with myself, and remembered my own click story as one which, purely and simply, grounded my politics in the personal.

Sitting with male friends one night at a bar when I was twenty-one, I made the acquaintance of an older, affable man, who had been buying rounds for the table. (By this age I had already been radicalized by reading – at seventeen I burned through Germaine Greer's *The Female Eunuch* in one sitting and proceeded to castigate every man I knew who hid back issues of *Playboy* in his closet.) This man eventually turned to me and told me a joke about a sex-change operation, the punch line being that a man would have to have half of his brain removed to become a woman. It was at that moment that my mental gears ground, producing the understanding that I was a woman, that I was *that* woman.

I demanded to know how he could tell me a joke like that, declaring that he would be lucky to have one-third of my brain. Actually I screamed at him, he cringed, and my friends berated me; after all, he was buying the drinks.

I have told this story to young women, students who begin sentences with the qualifier "I'm not a feminist, but. . . ." This year, I finally asked them why they were so reluctant to describe themselves as feminists, expecting to hear them make the uncomfortable equation of feminism with man-hating and unattractive plaid separates. They told me that they didn't know what it meant, that it seemed to mean many different things. After giving them my standard line, via Robin Morgan, that feminism exists wherever women meet and talk and testify, I thought that confusion is what we have inherited after the fact. After the clearly defined and follow-the-dots feminism of the second wave.

The program, as I understood it as a young woman, was imperative, exhilarating, and perfectly suited to those "thrill-seeking" women Valerie Solanis tried to recruit for SCUM. Like all movements that advocate change, however, feminism has had to expand to accommodate the difference and divergence of its constituents. And the confusion or chaos that is our legacy is equally electrifying, like surfing on a wider, less temperate sea. While I still define myself as a feminist as I understood it then – I am one of *them* – I find myself bound by the collective but also asserting, like a rake and miscreant, that "I don't want to be tied" to one way of thinking or another.

In this spirit, I solicited work for *Click* from a wide range of contributors, hoping to represent, in part, the epic numbers of women who contribute to the field of feminist discourse. Age, race, religion, class, and attitude are the most obvious variables: the women I approached were women I felt had distinguished themselves by enacting and inscribing feminism in their art and lives. I knew that their spins on the subject would vary wildly and was not disappointed when all of them responded as individuals within a shifting series of contexts. Mothers and daughters; the patriarch and the patriarchal; culture, society, and religion; beauty and horror; oppression and victory; sexuality and violence – these are some of the themes or backdrops that rattled into place behind the speakers.

The *Click* essays made me realize that the term not only resonates: it still provokes the kind of feminist truth-telling and problem-solving I have always looked to for solidarity and for answers. Each of these essays, ultimately, offers two narratives: the click, or understanding, that is embedded in one woman's experience; and the concomitant story, about ourselves.

The term *feminism* had lost its luster for me some time ago. The political sensibility I had acquired – once reckless and revolutionary – became as familiar to me, as ineluctable, as my gender. But as I read this completed anthology, I felt that old excitement return, an excitement I have always equated with learning, with discovery, with affirmation. An anthology is, by etymon, a "collection of flowers." And, as Aphra Behn observed in 1688, "For who that gathers the fairest flowers believes / A snake lies hid beneath the fragrant leaves." In its circular, sinuous fashion, feminism uncoils here, impressing its subtle, original sting.

My Life as a

Mamie Van Doren

is a Hollywood legend, best known for her screen-siren roles
in the 1950s films

High School Confidential,

Girls Town,

and *Untamed Youth.*

She is also the author of *Playing the Field* (1987), her memoirs.

She lives in California
and is working on a new book.

Decoration

MAMIE VAN DOREN

The movie scene in the 1950s was to feminism what a *cleaver* is to *meat*.

The studio system had been in charge of what audiences saw on the screen for thirty years. Precious few films of the period contain strong feminine characters because the studios – in concert with the half-assed piety and thinly veiled hypocrisy of the **CENSORSHIP boys** from the Johnson and Hays offices – created images of women dreamed up by men. There were **VERY FEW WOMEN** then in executive positions at the studio. There were no women as studio heads.

If you were an actress called upon to portray one of those images, you were required to live your life in accordance with the restrictions of that image – or else. There was **no tolerance** of illegitimate children, extramarital affairs, or nude layouts in men's magazines.

I did a photo layout for *Playboy* in 1963 that earned me the enmity of many in the Hollywood establishment. (It also earned me money. I had a young son to support.) Jayne Mansfield had done the same thing the year before with the identical result. This was many years, you will remember, before nude, pr**EGn**ant actresses would appear on the covers of women's magazines. (And more power to Demi Moore, believe me!)

My *Playboy* appearance subjected me to some shocking criticism. (Even today in America, the likes of Jerry Falwell and Janet Reno would propose a sort of **ethnic cleansing** of all who would create entertainments not blessed by them.) I was unexpectedly ostracized by people in the strangest quarters. The very men who would buy the magazine and gleefully jerk off to it would be damned if they would hire me for a role in a movie.

I envy women who are aware of the moment that they became feminists. It took a long time for feminism's revelations to come to me. My naive trust in the system of checks and balances would take years to erode. And in the meantime, I worked while the parasites became rich.

The studios packaged femininity to match what the public wanted. What did the public want? **SEX**, of course. But, after so many years of repression, we couldn't bring ourselves to call it what it was. We created instead a symbolic language – a visual language written in flesh. The metaphor we created was called the *Sex Symbol*, a theme that has run through movies since Theda Bara.

A star emerging from one studio had a **galvanizing** effect on the others. Marilyn Monroe's light winked on at 20th Century–Fox, and the other studios, seeing her popularity expressed in box office receipts, immediately began to develop their own "answers." Each studio began searching for its own dumb blonde. As luck would have it, Universal International decided that I was theirs. I became Universal's answer to Marilyn Monroe, though I (and they) had no idea what the real question was. It was the era of **Name Changing**: Rock, Tony, Tab, Piper, Mamie. They obliterated your identity by taking away your name. Thus came into being the so-called

CLICK TO

glAMour era of the 1950s in Hollywood. It was destined to be Hollywood's last.

Unfortunately, Universal was clueless when it came to developing female talent. They could build Rock Hudson or Tony Curtis into major stars, but they were baffled as to how to cultivate their actresses. It is difficult to name a woman of similar stature to Rock and Tony who emerged from that era at Universal.

To be fair (and not to bite the hand that fed me), I have to say the studio provided me with an **education** in the course of turning me into a so-called sex symbol. Universal was famous for its talent school. Of all the big studios, Universal had grasped the concept that the best-looking (and presumably the most talented) of the would-be actors and actresses *flock*ing to Hollywood could be trained. They developed into fairly competent performers and provided the studio with a virtually endless supply of talent for the scores of movies produced there every year. The talent school curriculum included classes in acting, diction, singing, dance, riding, and fencing. If, here and there, the occasional star emerged, so much the better. If not, they were at least **camera fodder** – walking, talking warm bodies who could people crowd scenes or deliver an occasional line. Eventually, if audiences didn't respond to certain contract players, their options would not be picked up and their careers at Universal would be quietly ended. There was never a shortage of new faces waiting to pass through that big studio gate on Lankershim Boulevard.

We, the sex goddesses, became a sort of **Castrati in the Movies** — a class of performers locked into our roles by our physical attributes. Who could imagine seeing Mamie Van Doren playing a nun? Who would want to? No, glamour girls were born to be glamour girls. When they could no longer be glamour girls, many found *life* unbearable. How many **succumbed** to overdoses? How many sought solace in drinking? How many lived their lives in Hollywood's ever-crowded fast lane until they met the *inevitable* head-on collision with death?

If you didn't die trying to **fulfill** someone else's idea of *womanhood*, you died when their idea no longer made sense in your life.

The studio sent you to **PREMIERES**, press **conferences**, and *Parties*, all with the purpose of garnering headlines. My first studio-arranged date was with

Rock Hudson. He took me to the Golden Globe Awards at the Beverly Hills Hotel. It was the most glamorous night of my life up to then, and I was happy to be there. Universal won coverage from columnists and wire services, newsreel footage, television, and radio. So did I. The exposure of a new starlet like me at an event of that caliber was one of the most helpful things imaginable for my career.

The quicker help came, the better. It was understood at the time that men aged gracefully, but women just lost their looks. Gable could play leading men until the day he died, but the likes of Bette Davis and Joan Crawford became character actresses. Not long after I got my contract at Universal, Bud Westmore, the movie makeup guru, said to me, "Mamie, you have ten years. Once you're thirty, you're over the hill." (Happily, thanks to loyal **FANS** who have helped give my movies **"cuLt"** status, I have had much more than Bud's allotted decade.)

There were other, less glamorous events that we starlets were expected to attend. It was not unusual to be asked to attend parties for visiting foreign dignitaries (even **Nikita Khrushchev** wanted to meet a movie star), corporate officers, and other VIPs visiting the studio. On one occasion I was sent to a party for the Shah of Iran. It was expected that we would take our time – after working hours – to get dolled up and trot off to some affair just to look pretty. There was no requirement that we go to bed with the guests of honour, but we were expected to be charming and a little bit dumb. Finally I refused to go unless I could bring my date (soon-to-be husband, bandleader Ray Anthony). When I did, they gave us a seat with the help.

The studios' concern about censorship led to ludicrous contradictions, and the more they tried to repress sexuality, the more it found expression in other ways. While they worried over the least show of cleavage, we padded our bullet bras and wore sweaters that presented our breasts as outsized cones. Faced with the problem of making a movie about Adam and Eve (*The Private Lives of Adam and Eve*) – sometime, somewhere **bare-assed** in the Garden of Eden – Universal's censors required that my breasts be covered by **flesh**-colored balloon rubber with hair extensions glued over them. If you **look closely** at the movie today, you'll see Marty Milner eyeing two enormous mounds of hair on my chest. And, because the censors fretted over the sight of my belly button, the makeup department glued my fig leaf slightly north of its traditional location. Marty's navel, of course, was there for all to see.

Just over the horizon was a decade in which **REpressION** would give way to liberation. Hastened by television, norms would be turned upside down, bras would be tossed away (thankfully!), and a new breed called the flower child would celebrate the body and spirit.

Sixties feminists looked with scorn on the glamour girls of the movies as symbols of sexual stereotypes established by the male power structure. They were right. I looked at the sixties **revolution** as a fearful time of change, yet a collective yearning to break out of the boring molds of the postwar fifties gave all of us a sense that something was **coming**. As **seX, dRUgs, & RoCk 'N' RoLL** became a part of our language, the covert titillation of the 1950s glamour era gave way to the unabashed hedonism of the 1960s.

Movies have always reflected the secret psyches of the audience. **Think** about what a sexist idea glamour is. **Men** find a woman attractive, and if she is not too smart, she is deemed glamorous. **Women** may agree that she is glamorous, but that is based on her desirability to men – a kind of acknowledgment of the competition. Now, no one said we had to compete, but who can **fight** the instinctual behavior of reproduction? No one said that women had to have their breasts pumped full of silicone, or their lips pumped full of fat, but many a tit and lip in this town has been enhanced because of the psychological pressure to compete.

Only the strongest could break away from the hold of the male-dominated studio system. In the end I broke away almost unconsciously – by having a baby. The studio made it clear that there was no room at Universal for a sex goddess who was married with children. The next thing I knew, I was a freelancer with a failed marriage and no alimony (I never asked), trying to support myself and my son. That was when I found out what feminism was really all about: **SURVIVAL**.

^aCLICK

Pat Califia
is a widely published leather dyke author whose fiction and
nonfiction frequently address feminist issues. Her most recent work includes *Public Sex*, a collection of essays about
radical sexual politics, and *Sex Changes*, a book about the
politics of transsexuality. She lives in San Francisco.

is a **noise** that a **woman** makes

PAT CALIFIA

A CLICK IS A NOISE that a woman makes with her tongue pressed against her front teeth. With her lips pursed, she makes a small private comment whenever she encounters something that depresses, discourages, or disgusts her, and knows she is likely to encounter it again. She tsk-tsks at other people's dirty clothes left on the floor, a check that bounced because her husband did not write down an ATM transaction, a child's smashed-up toy.

That little noise is one of only partial resignation. It says: *I am still enough of a person to notice this indignity. I do not accept it blindly as my lot. I remark upon it, and reproach you.* But it is also a sort of surrender, a way of pointing out misdeeds without actually objecting to them or asking anyone to change.

It is a sound that I often heard my mother make, to herself, but pitched to carry to the rest of the family. It filled me with guilt, dread, pity, and anger. I never wanted to be like her, stooped over somebody else's mess and not doing anything about it except making that carping little noise. I did not want to keep my teeth together or my tongue behind them, and I loathed the look of her pinched-up mouth, its curses smugly withheld. From childhood, I was rowdy with indignation. If the world did me an injustice, I thought my teeth should be exposed in an honest growl. In fact, I never wanted to be a child at all. I was frantic to grow up, always pushing for more freedom, always looking for a way to escape from my raging father and my fanatically Mormon mother and the damage they did to my younger siblings.

But I *was* a child, a state that is perhaps inherently unhappy. And there were limits placed upon me – my physical size, the expectations of other people, church and school and the complex emotional and physical boundaries that regulate small-town life. What I could not evade, I endured. But that did not mean I had to see things the same way that other people saw them. I split myself in two, a public self that did the minimum amount of conforming necessary to survive and a secret self that watched, judged, and remembered.

I went to school and got good grades. I put myself in the path of my father's anger to divert him away from my mother and my brothers and sisters – rubbing his back, sitting with him while he watched television so he would not have to change his own channels, rising to his bait during dinner so that no one else would get insulted or slapped. My mother took us to church twice a week, and I went along, having about as much choice as a car being towed.

But my real self kept score. When my father would say, "Don't use that tone of voice with me. I am your father, and you had damn well better respect me," I said, "Yes, sir," but inside I knew he was wrong to show his anger so freely. I knew that no one could force me to respect them; I knew that a parent's job is to love, not to intimidate or batter. When my mother would appropriate my notebooks and upbraid me for the bad language or dangerous ideas she found written down in my hand, I would nod and nod, and as soon as she let me go, I would find a better hiding place for my work. I learned how to keep what was really important to me locked in my memory. Someday, I hoped, it would be safe to spill it onto an empty page.

Hiding is a lonely strategy, and of course it was not entirely successful. I frequently thought I was crazy or destined for hell. It was poor camouflage, besides. Even a pack of feral dogs recognizes a wolf and knows it is not a brother, not a potential member of the pack. In a fundamentalist Christian community, it doesn't take much defiance to set off fireworks. Other people, at school, at church, on the street, knew I was not safe to be around. I was the little girl who fought back on the playground, the straight-A student who was always getting detention for sassing the teachers, the teenager who said she was never going to get married. (People pointed me out in church for that piece of my reputation.)

Within my secret and silenced self, I became aware that there are also clicks that nobody else hears, a "sound" that your consciousness makes when it registers a dissonance between the meaning that everyone else seems to be assigning to an event, and the meaning that it holds for you. During those long years of incarceration within my nuclear family and their strange religion, I had so many clicks going off in my soul that I felt like a Geiger counter lost in the bowels of a uranium mine.

Despite my vow to remember everything, which I swore with as much passion as a Mafia princess swears vengeance, I'm sure many of those moments are lost beyond recall. And a few of the things I remember with such fervor quite probably never happened at all. We're all fiction writers, in a way, because we are constantly telling ourselves the story of our own lives. The urge to create a narrative seems to be a building block of human consciousness. When raw data are handled by imagination and the hidden needs of the subconscious, they are transformed into cautionary tales, heroic quests, horror stories, and epics of true love. The past polishes up better than sterling silver. Still, these are the treasures I keep from that time, my inaudible gasps of protest. They are so much a part of who and why I am that I cannot help but defend them as the gospel truth, even if it is only a metaphorical sort of veracity.

IN FIRST GRADE, I came home crying because a boy at school had pulled my long, beloved braid so hard that my scalp still hurt. My mother laughed and said, "That's how you can tell that boys like you." The next time it happened, I turned around and punched my tormentor in the mouth, knocking out one of his teeth. I wound up in the principal's office, and my mother cut off my hair. *Oh no*, I thought, *something is very wrong here. Why didn't anybody say, "That's how you can tell that girls like you"?*

WHEN REPORT CARDS CAME, we had to show them to my father that evening, so that he could sign them. It was such a tense occasion that it made me sick to my stomach. He would prolong the anxiety by waiting until the last minute to announce whether we were supposed to visit him in the order of youngest to eldest, or the reverse. I never got anything lower than a B plus, but my father was always incensed at my report card. He believed there was no excuse for anything other than an A. On one occasion, I was able to present him with a perfect (I thought) report card. His response was to give me a withering look and announce, "Well, you'll never have much of a social life. Boys really don't like girls who are smart." In a flash I understood that I would always be wrong. I would always be told that I had to try harder, achieve more, but if I succeeded, my victory would be held against me.

MY MOTHER DECIDED when we reached a certain age that it was time for all of us to do chores. She drew up a chart. We would take turns cleaning the bathroom, doing dishes, ironing, and dusting. Only her daughters' names appeared on the chart. I pitched a fit. "But these are girls' jobs," my mother said.

"Boys need to know how to do housework too," I countered. "They won't always be married." Then inspiration struck. "When they are missionaries," I said, desperate to win this fight, "they will have to look after themselves for two whole years!"

My mother gave me a look that said, *I have nursed a viper in my bosom*, and added mowing the lawn and taking out the trash to the chart. Those jobs were allocated to my brothers. The only concession she would make was in the realm of ironing, because I absolutely refused to iron my brothers' clothes. "But I've ironed your clothes all these years," she said sadly, inviting me to join a selfless sisterhood of domestic service.

"I don't care," I said. "I'm not doing it. It's wrong."

"I can't believe you are making such a big deal out of a little housework," my mother said, getting angry.

k

I stopped answering her back, but inside, I thought this could not be such a trivial thing if we had to fight about it. The world was organized so that women did other people's shit work. This system was so important that not even one adolescent girl could be allowed to refuse to participate in it. It wasn't optional, it was compulsory; and it wasn't natural, or I would not have hated the very idea of it.

Even when he was unemployed, my father refused to let my mother get a job outside the home. When he had once been without work for almost a year, and we were eating toast for dinner, my mother shamed him into taking a job he did not want by going to work in a sewing factory. It was my job to cook dinner while she was coming home from the factory, and most nights my father refused to eat anything I had cooked because I was not his wife and it was not my job to make his supper. The atmosphere in the house was wretched. It was the closest he ever came to hitting his wife instead of his children. He finally gave in, called his friend in another state, and got a job. The day we took him to the airport was one of the happiest days of my life.

But the fact that my mother did not have a job did not mean that she had no work. She worked constantly. She had six children. I saw her make three meals every day for eight people, do laundry every day, wash dishes, clean the house, sew our clothes for school, make small repairs around the house, put up jam and can fruit, shop for groceries, help us with our homework. She hardly ever sat down. If she tried to read a book, one of us would interrupt her. The only place where she could escape was to church, and she did a lot of volunteer work for the church.

Despite the enormous effort it took to keep the household running, my father said to her, at least once a week, "Well, what did you do all day, watch soap operas on television?"

Women's work, I learned, is invisible. Men would do almost anything to avoid doing women's work, but that did not mean they were grateful to women for taking care of it. Sadly, I never felt much gratitude to my mother for her constant care and bustle. I thought it was stupid of her to have so many children, stupid of her to give her life to so much drudgery and repetitive, idiotic chores. *Not me*, I vowed, *not me!*

This aversion was enhanced by the Mormon doctrine that earthly marriage continues in the hereafter. Families are sealed to one another for time and all eternity. Time and all eternity! What a joke. I knew I couldn't bear to do what wives and mothers did for five minutes.

WHEN I HIT PUBERTY (or rather, it hit me), my body changed so fast that I had growing pains shooting up and down my arms and legs. My senses became incredibly keen, and all my emotions were intensified. The world was a place of infinitely more beauty and terror. These changes took a lot of energy. There wasn't a moment when I wasn't ravenous. My mother decided that this was a good time to put me on a diet, to keep me from getting fat. I was five-foot-two and weighed 130 pounds. The rest of the family would eat chicken and mashed potatoes and gravy, and I had a salad. The only way I got through this was to sneak downstairs in the middle of the night and make myself hot cocoa and french fries, then carefully and silently clean up all traces of my feast.

The next day, I would sit in the school cafeteria and watch boys my own age wolf down huge trays full of food. More often than not, they would get up, get their lunch tickets punched again, and go through the line for a second helping of everything. The ladies who served us lunch would smile at them and make glowing comments about growing boys. I wanted to kill them all.

That rage could not save me from the conviction that I was fat as a dumpling and plain as a blackboard. This was the sixties, and we were all supposed to look like Twiggy. I had the short, stocky, powerful body that made it possible for my Welsh forebears to drag tons of coal out of the earth or hoist bales of hay from a hundred acres. I was in danger of becoming a bulimic, although nobody knew that word then, but I was rescued by a conversation with a beautiful girl who was three years older than me.

We wound up talking into the wee hours at 4-H camp. There is something about total darkness and the cocoon of a sleeping bag that encourages confidences. She was everything I wanted to be: tall, slim, with long, straight blonde hair and beautifully kept hands with long, polished fingernails. She told me that her hands were hurting her so much she couldn't sleep, because of the medicine she put on them to get rid of warts. She hated her hands. She hated her hands so much it made her cry. I comforted her, and she went to sleep, and then I lay there in the dark thinking about all the pretty girls I knew who thought they were fat, or hated their noses, or were self-conscious about their skin. It was always something, a big butt, a flat chest, skinny calves, split ends, tearing at us, ripping apart our self-esteem, making us insecure and needy for compliments. *But we're fine just the way we are*, I thought. *Women are beautiful just the way they are. I don't want to play this game.*

ONE OF THE ADVANTAGES of growing up in a fundamentalist religion is the clarity. There's no liberal gloss, none of this stuff about God transcending gender or ordaining the occasional gay priest. We were told, in simple terms that nobody could misunderstand, that women were created to be subservient to men. God talked to men, who held the priesthood, and they supervised us, and we did not hold the priesthood.

By eavesdropping on adult conversations about the esoterica of Mormon doctrine, I gathered that we were supposed to have a mother, as well as a father, in heaven. I once asked my mother, while we were all kneeling for prayer before dinner, why we never prayed to our mother in heaven. She was completely taken aback at the idea. Finally she stammered something about how our mother in heaven is too sacred to be mentioned out loud, and it was important to keep her hidden so that people would not take her name in vain.

Give me a break, I thought. What kind of god is unable to receive devotion or intercede for those who petition for her blessing? Was God's wife as impotent to protect me as my mother was? Or was it just that they didn't want us to really know about her and worship her, for fear she would get to be too powerful? That made a lot more sense to me, and I started addressing my evening prayers to a female deity that very evening.

My poor mother knew that I was not going to grow up like all her other children. I kept telling everyone who would listen that I was not going to get married when I grew up, because I did not want some man to have control over my life, and I did not want children. Despite that heretical announcement, my mother kept trying to find a place for me in her world. Her response to my bookishness was to encourage me to be a schoolteacher. And her response to my discontent with Mormon theology was to encourage me to read the scriptures and go on a mission. That was, she said, almost as good as having the priesthood.

This backfired when I found out that Joseph Smith, the founder of the Mormon church, had ordained his wife Emma. This story was in the *Doctrine and Covenants*, one of the unique books that Mormons value as scripture along with the Bible which other Christians recognize. I took this to my mother, who read it with her lips pursed. She was too upset to tsk at me. "Joseph only ordained Emma because she had a rebellious spirit, and she drove him crazy with her questions and her complaints," she declared. "It wasn't meant to set a precedent."

I decided to take the book to my Sunday School teacher, who might know more about this than my mother, or even ask the bishop. But on Sunday when I went looking for my copy of the book, it was gone. "You read too much," my mother told me. "You also talk too much. Try listening in church for a change."

ONE DAY in my early teens I decided that it was time to ask my mother about sex. So I confronted her after dinner. She did not want to talk about it. "Don't they teach you this in school?" she asked weakly. That was a joke. My mother would have been in the vanguard of a parental movement to oppose sex education, if there had been any. Then she ran away and got some drawing paper and pencils. She came back to the kitchen table and tried to draw something, then gave that up and tried to say something. This was unbelievably painful to watch, but I kept biting my tongue. I would not let her off the hook. I wanted to know; it was her job to tell me.

Finally she gave up and said, "I'm really sorry. My own mother never talked to me about this, and I always thought I would do better than that with my own children. But I will get some information for you. I promise."

A few days later, she gave me a booklet. It had diagrams of the reproductive organs and a sparse, clinical description of intercourse, conception, and fetal development. I looked at the pictures, read the words, and tried to figure out why anybody would want to do this. I knew there had to be much more than this. They were leaving out something that was important. But what?

I studied the booklet for clues until it was in danger of falling apart. Then my mother confiscated it. This information was not mine, it did not belong to me, it was on loan, and it was (like my sexuality) supposed to remain under her control until I passed into the control of a husband. I could not believe that my mother thought I had now received adequate information to prepare me for marriage, sex, and childbirth. Ignorance, I realized, was as important as virginity, for exactly the same reasons.

Later, when I found out what was missing from that booklet, I was furious. There was nothing in it about love or pleasure. Nothing about masturbation, the clitoris, or female orgasms. Nothing about sexual fantasies. No whisper of any alternative to monogamous heterosexuality and reproductive sex. I had wasted years of my adolescence feeling like I must be the most bizarre person in the world, that nobody else masturbated or saw the things I saw when I made myself come. Well, maybe boys did, but not other girls. My mother was supposed to love me, but she would not have cared if I lived my whole life without ever experiencing an orgasm. She would not have thought it was important.

I dated only one boy in high school, and he spent every minute we were alone together pressuring me to have sex with him. There was no possibility of using birth control. As teenagers, we simply didn't have access to it. No pharmacist would have sold him condoms, and even if I had somehow managed to sneak away from my family or school and visit Planned Parenthood, there was no way I could hide birth control pills or a diaphragm from my mother. I already knew girls who had left high school because they were pregnant, and that was not going to happen to me. I tried to explain some of this to him, and quickly found out that I might as well have been speaking Martian. "I would never do anything to hurt you," he said, while trying to ruin my life.

The physical pain of unsatisfied adolescent lust is very difficult to bear. One day I let him put his hands inside my clothing. After that date, he said, "I have to tell you that I really don't respect you any more. When can I see you again?"

"Never," was my reply. My own hands did not have a lot of surprises for me, and it is impossible to kiss yourself. But I could do without the small and sweaty pleasures he gave me if it meant I did not need to listen to his double-talk and add his condemnation to my own guilt about being a sexual person. There had to be a better way to express these feelings, experience these sensations. Unfortunately, by the time I found a safer place to be sexual, with other women, the adolescent piquancy of my need was gone. What could have been one of the most wonderful sexual phases of my life was stolen from me because I lived in a society that enforced ignorance of women's bodies, denied young people access to birth control, and relied on teenage indiscretion to trick us into a lifetime of marital obligations.

Our alienation from our own bodies is an even more cruel theft than the robbery of our time (to scrub other people's floors and wipe their brats' noses) or the hijacking of our affections (for men who fear and hate us, and more often than not feel free to ridicule and beat us). What kind of world would we live in if women controlled their own time, their own hearts, their own sexuality? It is feminism's task to answer that question.

WHEN I WAS ABOUT 14, my father decided my problem was that I was trying to be a boy. He would help me, he determined, by proving to me that I wasn't cut out to be a man. This meant that family games of touch football became tackle football. I also got boxing lessons. If I got hurt and I cried, my father would crow. "Boys don't cry," he would jeer. "You aren't as tough as you think you are. Why don't you go inside and knit a sweater?"

Sometimes my verbal battles with my father would turn into screaming matches that lasted for hours. I hated him so much that I could not control myself. I hated him for the atmosphere of fear that he created in our house, and I hated him for making my mother so financially dependent on him that she could not leave him. I especially hated being told that as long as my father put food on the table, he was doing a much better job than his own father had, and so we had no right to complain.

After particularly evil battles, it was my father's way to insist that I accompany him downstairs to the family room, where we would break down and clean his extensive collection of pistols and rifles. I loved the smell of gun oil, and there was something fascinating about the feel of cold blue metal. I sometimes stole bullets to keep under my tongue, for the metallic thrill of their taste. But I hated being his companion under duress, having to follow his directions, never being able to perform a task to his satisfaction, and getting cuffed for my errors.

During one of these sessions, he laughed at me and said, handing me a pistol, "I'll bet there are times when you'd like to shoot your old man. Just sneak downstairs in the middle of the night and – boom! – blow him away. But you won't, you know. Because you don't have the guts for it. It takes a man to decide he's had enough, to stand up and fight back. Give me another patch for this barrel."

I don't think I slept at all that night. I lay on my back shaking, my teeth locked together, staring at the ceiling while beads of cold sweat formed on my face and the palms of my hands. I knew how those guns worked. He had insisted on teaching me how the guns worked. I could do it. I could go downstairs, I knew how to step on each stair without making it squeak. I knew where the ammunition was. I could load the smallest pistol, and take it into the bedroom, and make him disappear.

There would be blood everywhere. My mother would never forgive me. Some of the blood would get on her. Some of it would probably get on me, too, but that didn't bother me. Then they would come for me and lock me up. And they would never let me go. It wouldn't matter that he had humiliated and hurt us. Even if he came at me to kill me, I suddenly realized, I couldn't fight back. I would always be the criminal, if I raised my hand against my father.

Now that was a click that I could not figure out how to accommodate by shifting my own consciousness. That was an indignity too huge for me to handle by splitting into my secret self and my public self. The world would have to change, that was all. The whole world would have to change to right that wrong.

THEN, I did not know that I was going to leave home at seventeen, become a dyke, move to San Francisco, start writing banned books, and eventually help to found a politically aware S/M community. I would have laughed at the thought that someday I would be grateful for the strength, determination, and practicality my family and the Mormon church had given me. All I knew was that the world was in turbulence, and I was barred from participation in this sea change. Even the bowdlerized evening news and newspapers that we got in Utah could not hide the fact that people were protesting against the war in Vietnam, advocating free love, doing LSD, developing a youth culture, and creating music that shook the foundations of every institution. The only thing that kept me at home was a lack of money and a fear that if I ran away, I would not survive. As a working-class person, I would always remember that money is the basis for freedom. Without cash, you can't take care of yourself or your friends, and you can't afford to be different.

I had a small savings account. My mother had opened savings accounts for all of us as soon as we were old enough to recognize different kinds of coins and count to 100. We were, however, only supposed to put money in, not take it out. I disobeyed this dictum twice, and they were both very important moments for me, because they were harbingers of a time when all my money (and every other resource I might have) would be in my own two hands.

The first transgression was to take out ten dollars to give to a classmate so she could mail-order a deck of tarot cards for me. I don't remember how I hid them from my mother, who would certainly have seized them and burned them as Satan's handmaidens if she'd ever known I had them. I still have that deck today. It was thrilling to read the little brochure that came with them and realize that these images had been painted by a Victorian woman. Even then, some women found a way to do something besides dishes and child care. There were so many important messages that came to me from those vibrantly colored cards: the knowledge that there was a spirituality that had nothing to do with organized religion, images of powerful women – queens and goddesses, validation for my intuition and the non-rational parts of my psyche, proof that women could make art and have it survive and influence others. The tarot was a gateway for me into the future. It said: *Imagination and beauty are just as important as hard work and cynicism. You don't have to be a farmer's wife or a suicide. Somewhere in the world there is room for people like you.*

My second fiscal transgression took place when I saw a copy of Betty Friedan's book *The Feminine Mystique* on the single rack of paperback books in the drugstore on Main Street. I got up early to catch a ride into town with my dad so I could go to the bank and take out money. When I sneaked into the drugstore and grabbed the only copy of the book that they had, I was afraid they would not sell it to me. And, in fact, the woman at the cash register thought about it. She picked up the book and looked at it, pursed her lips, and looked at me.

But this was a waitress who had served my dad coffee (which Mormons are not supposed to drink) and joked with him about his uptight wife. My mother reacted to my dad's weekly trip into town for a cup of coffee the way most women react to the news that their husbands are having an affair. Waitresses were just one step up from prostitutes in her mind. Maybe it pleased the working woman behind the counter to see me going bad. Whatever her motivation, she sold me the book and walked away looking a little disturbed about her decision, shaking her head and clicking her tongue. I ran out of there before she could change her mind.

In later years when I was a part of the women's movement and Friedan became infamous for her opposition to lesbians becoming more visible as feminists, I had a hard time hating her, because that book saved my life. Here was a calm, rational, educated woman presenting clear facts about why "normal," "feminine" roles drove women crazy, cheated us of our potential to be whole human beings, and damaged our minds and bodies. *The Feminine Mystique* became a new sort of scripture for me. Until I could actually meet other feminists and talk to them, it became my consciousness-raising group, my lifeline, yet another vision of the future. It also taught me that the ideas in books go where people cannot.

Like my tarot cards, Friedan's book was in danger of going up in flames along with the trash my mother burned every week in an empty oil barrel in our backyard. I had to keep it in my locker at school and read it only between classes to keep it out of the hands of adults who would have destroyed it. And so I became a protector of the fragile printed page, a knight-errant wearing the favor of Lady Heresy, prepared to do battle with censorship or any other limit on free expression. Because without the right to imagine social change, discuss it, and advocate for it, women will remain chattels. No matter how it is dressed up as a bid to protect us, suppression of any form of media will have negative repercussions for women. We have no right more important or more precarious than our right to simply speak our minds.

makes

piecing together a childhood:

LORNA CROZIER

T HE MOST POWERFUL FIGURE in my childhood was my mother. I can't begin to describe all that she taught me, but it's easy to list some of the advice she passed on. Rub goose grease on your throat and chest to stop a cold, don't put your shoes on the table or you'll bring bad luck, and don't take shit from men. In talking with some of my friends, I've discovered that this last bit of wisdom is a fairly common one. It crosses all kinds of borders. Perhaps that's because being female and growing up poor create other commonalities that bridge the distances between different cultures and racial backgrounds, like my friend Louise's and mine.

Louise says her great mentor was her Nokum. A Cree medicine woman, her teachings were respected on the reserve: swallow skunk oil to cure whooping cough, burn sweetgrass to get rid of bad spirits, and don't take shit from men. After her grandmother died, Louise's mother repeated the old woman's warning. These days, however, when she visits her daughter, she speaks only of the lizards in her head. That's how she sees her pain, Louise says, sharp-clawed reptiles with fiery tongues and long thrashing tails. Years ago they crawled behind

one
feminist's
beginnings

Lorna Crozier's

poetry has been translated into several languages and widely published in magazines and anthologies. Her book *Inventing the Hawk* (1992) received the Governor General's Award, the Pat Lowther Award for best book of poetry by a Canadian woman, and the Canadian Authors Association Literary Award. *A Saving Grace: The Collected Poems of Mrs. Bentley* was published by McClelland & Stewart in 1996. Lorna Crozier lives in British Columbia with the poet Patrick Lane and teaches writing at the University of Victoria.

her eyes after one too many beatings; her husband's kicks and punches shaking the walls of the cabin, Louise and her siblings hiding under the bed. "Don't take shit from men."

Unlike Louise's, my father didn't beat my mom. "If he ever hit me," she said, "he knows he'd be out the door." She was a strong, fiercely proud young woman, yet one of my sharpest memories is of her begging for grocery money, Dad holding out a dollar bill. "That's not enough," she would say, knowing he'd spent five times that amount at the beer parlor the night before. Eventually he'd open his wallet and tease her with another dollar just beyond her reach. It was a game he liked to play.

She ended up cleaning house for two lawyers' wives so she wouldn't have to ask him again. "Best thing that ever happened to me," she tells me now. "I saw how the other half lived and it wasn't worth much." When I was seven, she got her first real job, selling tickets and checking baskets full of clothing at the swimming pool. My father fumed around the house for days. He didn't want anyone thinking he couldn't support his family. I didn't understand.

There was not a moment of conversion, a "click" of sudden insight that turned me into a feminist. There was a whole childhood with its chaos, contradictions, and amazing ambiguities, with its fragments I need to stitch together to make a whole. There was my own sense of injustice. There was my family.

Always an observer, I stood outside myself and watched, often raging quietly inside, often huddled in my bedroom, singing out loud so I could block the voices on the other side of the wall, the endless nightly bickering, the curses my drunken father hurled at Mom. I imagined the words were thick black bugs chewing through the plaster to the wall above my bed, and I smashed them with my fists. Why did he have to come home like that? Why did she have to berate him? Couldn't she just pretend to be asleep? Why did he have to come home at all?

The next morning, not wanting to sit at the breakfast table in the middle of their terrible silence, I'd say "I'm not hungry" and run out to play. I loved them both dearly and I hated them. I couldn't understand why my mother took it. After all, she told me not to. What was wrong with her? Nor could I delight in her verbal thrashing of him when he was weak, when he sat at the table ashamed of being out of work, the oil fields closed for the winter once again. His hand shook as he tried to move his spoon from the sugar bowl to his cup. When I did sit between them at breakfast, I stared at the trail of sugar he had spilled, imagined the three of us reflected over and over in each facet of the crystals, our faces multiplied to infinity: my father, mother, and I trapped in the sharp-edged sweetness of family.

How many times did I watch my mother iron his clothes – even his handkerchiefs and underwear – wash his hair, pack his black tin lunch bucket, keep his supper warm on the back of the stove long after she and I had grown tired of waiting and had finished eating? Sunday afternoons I watched her clean the fish thrashing in the pail he had carried to the house from the speedboat she hadn't wanted him to buy. Sometimes she made him take me boating, and we roared back and forth at Duncaren Dam, the waves lifting us and banging us down. The motion had something to do with the way I was feeling; it had something to do with our lives. I had no words for it then.

Mid-afternoon, he'd stop close to shore and we'd eat lunch in the boat, the waves rocking us gently. With the chicken sandwiches Mom had made, butter melting into the white bread, he'd drink three beers, tilt the empty bottles in the water till they filled, and I'd watch them sink. "Don't tell your mother," he'd say. After he'd had enough of fishing, perch flipping the sunlight on the bottom of the boat, he'd let me slide over the edge and put on the water skis. The sixty-horse-power Evinrude pulled me upright like a new creature rising from the deep, Dad swerving back and forth across the wake. It was a game that pleased him, that made him feel proud of me when he couldn't make me tumble, the skis rattling under my feet like machine-gun fire. Sometimes he'd stop the motor and I'd fall in.

When we got home, Mom would sit on the back step, gutting and filleting, beside her my father nursing his last warm beer. Her hands and forearms were streaked with thin blood and slime, scales glinting bright as sequins, her mouth held tight. I stood to the side in my young girl's rage inventing what I'd say to them. I vowed I would never be like them; I vowed I would never clean fish for anyone. How wonderful it must have been to feel such pure and perfect anger, such youthful superiority. My mother slit the bellies, my father sipped, I held my righteous tongue.

So often I see only the three of us in scenes like this, as if I were an only child, but I have a brother. Seven years older than me, for almost half my life at home, he was gone, at first off to farm camps for the NHL, later to a boot camp in Petawawa. He was big, smart, and athletic, and as a kid I worshipped him. When I was little and couldn't be on my own with my friends and our dolls or Dinky toys, my mother would make him take me along in his treks through the neighborhood. "Let's play hide-and-seek," he'd say, and I'd run off while he turned his back and counted to ten. I'd hunch in the tall brome grass behind our backyard, close my eyes so no one could see me, dozens of grasshoppers snapping through the air. I didn't know he was off with his friends down at the creek where they caught frogs, leeches, and thin ribbons of garter snakes to wind around their wrists. What seemed like hours later, I'd hear my mother calling from the house and I'd go in for lunch, my brother already at the table, milk in his glass and along his upper lip. "You're so good at that," he'd say. "I couldn't find you." He was the one who counted. I, the one who hid.

If anyone had been looking, it would have been easy to find me then, but by the time I got to high school, I was doing my best to disappear from the family. For four years my brother had been gone, married and living with his wife and baby on the East Coast, not even returning for Christmas, not wanting to. I had stopped going off with Dad in the boat, and he spent more and more time in the Legion or at the Imperial, Healey, and York hotels. Twice he lost his driver's license, getting permission from the judge to operate only the Cat in the oil patch so he wouldn't be out of work. One of the other men on the site picked him up every morning and brought him home where he changed into clean clothes and a tie, always a tie, then left for a night of playing pool and shuffleboard.

Mom was leading what could have been called an independent life, if any of us had known the phrase, selling tickets for the Bronco Hockey Club in the winter, for the swimming pool in summer. Though there wasn't much money, she and Dad had separate bank accounts. She paid for groceries; he, for heat; and they split the rent. Everything I needed, she supplied. She took in boarders, continued to do day work as it was called, skipped a curling team, bowled once a week, and never asked for help with the cooking, cleaning, washing, and ironing. Nor did I offer. The epithet Superwoman for mothers like her had not yet been invented.

I was busy doing my best to be popular, to wear the right clothes, to straighten my hair by Scotch-taping my bangs to my forehead and winding long strands in painful brush rollers every night. For months, I tossed my head on the pillow in agony until I learned to sleep on my face. I was doing my best to say the right things, to tell nobody what I really thought or felt. "Don't take shit from men," my mother said. "And don't get pregnant."

When my period had started a few years before, she had ordered a booklet from Kotex called *You're a Young Lady Now*. On the cover a young girl with a ponytail, hair perfectly straight, gazed into a mirror. What I remember best about the book is its list of the things a girl with her period shouldn't do: don't go swimming, don't ride horseback, don't jump, don't run. All she could do, it seemed, was bathe, bathe, bathe.

Translating my mother's warning about men into "Don't put your-self at the mercy of *one* of them," when I started dating, I juggled two or three boys at a time. I wore one's hockey jacket, and when he left town for training camp, accepted his best friend's ring made smaller with a wad of adhesive tape wound around the silver. Three years run-ning I got a role in the operetta through sheer energy and force of will, for I couldn't sing. Mad to keep busy and out of the house, in Grade Eleven, I became captain of the cheerleading team. Since I couldn't turn a cartwheel, I had to develop another skill. Within a week, I be-came irreplaceable as the writer of all the yells and songs.

With the power bestowed ephemerally on an author, I insisted we chant the words in deep voices to distinguish us from the cheerleaders from the rich kids' school. Their voices were high and squeaky. We didn't want to sound like bimbos even though we may have looked like ones. Dressed in short, flippy skirts, we shook our pompoms in the gym that smelt of sex and sweat, our running shoes dyed in my mother's canner to match our uniform's bright blue. As the season progressed, our knees and elbows turned orange with the Quicktan we smeared on our winter-pale legs and arms. That year "California Girl" was the most popular Beach Boys song.

Yet we wanted to be taken seriously. We shopped in Woolworth's for bras that would stop the jiggling when we ran onto the field or court. We shouted and sang in the lowest registers, even when the boys from the basketball team said they'd kill us if we kept it up and if we didn't stop singing those stupid songs. If I had known the word *feminist* then, I would have used it in the argument we were having with them and their coach. We didn't take shit.

To be fair to my mother, she also said "Don't give up" and "Stand up for yourself." She said this to my brother when she couldn't afford to buy him shin pads for his first hockey games, and he came home bruised and sore to tears. She said it to me when I failed my first begin-ners' swimming test, partly because my feet couldn't reach the bottom in the three-foot-six shallow end and I was scared to let go of the edge. My brother almost made it to the NHL; I became a lifeguard; my mother has said "Don't give up" every time I've needed help in my life.

To be fair to my mother *and* father, she also said good things about him. He was never lazy, he was a wonderful dancer, he was good with his hands, even in the worst of times he thought something would turn up. "There's no one better," she said, "when he's sober." A few years ago when we scattered his ashes over the alkali lake on the farm where she grew up, she threw what little was left of him into the wind, and much to my surprise, called, "There you go! You made my life bet- ter." Later, I had to ask her what she meant. "He always told me to stand up for myself," she said. "I'd have had nothing if it wasn't for him." The confusing ambiguities of childhood continue in all their wonder.

My feminism comes out of these perplexing childhood experiences and more. For me, feminism is not a theory, but a way of living one's day-to-day life, its origins made up of incidents and observations stitched together. Some of them remain such odd shapes it's difficult to make them fit, these old scraps of cloth that I recognize, that I wore with shame or joy. Above my desk I've taped a quotation that circu- lated around women's groups a decade ago. Attributed simply to "a pioneer woman," it reads: "We had to make the quilts fast so the chil- dren wouldn't freeze. We had to make them beautiful so our hearts wouldn't break."

I've never made such a quilt nor has my mother, nor has my friend Louise, but there's one taking shape in my mind. Running my fingers across the different textures, smooth or nubby, I feel anger, I smile, I cry. There's a swatch of my first wool coat and my cheerleading skirt, a fragment of my mother's blue velvet wedding dress, a pocket-sized piece from my brother's hockey sweater, the point of my father's yel- low tie. My mother's phrases, *Don't give up*, *Stand up for yourself*, *Don't take shit from men*, are embroidered around the edge. Worked into the border are other words I came to much later in life, words I learned from reading such writers as Margaret Laurence, Doris Lessing, Alice Munro, Germaine Greer, Margaret Atwood, Adrienne Rich. Their books helped me understand what it was I was feeling all those years. In some ways, they have provided the thread that holds everything to- gether, making of these various pieces a whole. Something that has weight, something that has beauty, something I keep adding to though my fingers are clumsy, the stitches uneven. Something that my body knows. The thread breaks when I tug too hard and pieces often over- lap. Many times I prick my fingers on the needle and stain the worn familiar cloth with specks of blood.

THE TURNING POINT

KEMBRA PFAHL

Kembra Pfahler

has worked as an actress, a professional dominatrix, an S/M movie star, a coloring-book illustrator, a high-fashion model, a performance artist, and a writer. She is the founder and lead singer for the New York–based rock band The Voluptuous Horror of Karen Black. She is the president and owner of an all-women wrestling foundation (PLOW: Punk Ladies of Wrestling); she has recently been photographed for *Penthouse* magazine; and she is working on a book of photographs. Pfahler is also a filmmaker whose work has been screened at the Whitney Museum; she is currently working on a new film about her band.

I am neither boy or girl or something in between. Aliens, goblins, monster screams, we're the third kind or so that's what it seems.

— The Voluptuous Horror of Karen Black

THERE HAS NEVER BEEN one distinct "click" for me necessarily, although there has been a series of turning points, something like waking up suddenly and discovering you've been dead, and living like a ghost. I don't like imprisoning categories: if they were erased, maybe we could allow ourselves to be more perverse. I don't know exactly why I do what I do, and if I did, it would be pitiful to say so. I think of horror as a reflection and interpretation of the world that I see, which is ugly. The truth is ugly, but, like that old saying, it will set you free. It is this aesthetic that I approach in my work, as a way of creating and, because my medium is public, sharing artificial glamour. I have always felt more like a criminal or a soldier than an artist, but this is slowly changing. The vocabulary of images that I have developed through the band and through movies is a language that is not always spoken and, in my experience, not always paid for, but – oh well . . . attrition is the best revenge.

I grew up in South Bay, southern California. I used to buy twenty-five cents worth of candy on my way to the beach in the mornings: watermelon Jolly Ranchers, apple Jolly Ranchers, and Tootsie Rolls. Our moms made up a tackle line of backrests sitting along the waterfront, the gorgeous South Bay Pacific Ocean to which there is no comparable body of water in the world. The South Bay was what dreams were made of, what the Beach Boys wrote about. We ate clam chowder at night at the Mermaid Restaurant. Our parents went to the Lighthouse Bar while we snuck out and played under the pier or built forts under porches. I stared at the ocean for hours on my stomach, pulling the warm sand up to my chest, wearing my usual daytime outfit, an orange-and-pink Hawaiian-print pair of bikini bottoms. Squinting my eyes, peeling my nose, and chewing gum. Very seriously assessing the waves. This is exactly what my dad did as a world-renowned surfer. He and I lay down like that, looking at the ocean, not talking at all.

One day in August, around six o'clock, a bunch of us were going in the water for the last time, before we went home to dinner. About seven of us were bodysurfing the same wave in, getting thrown on our backs and upside down. Everybody standing up with their hair in their faces – you have to stick your head in again and flick your head back to get a good post-waterlog hairdo. As I was doing this and wiping my salty eyes I noticed all the kids standing around me yelling. "You're a girl, Kembra! You should wear a top!" My stomach sank and I suddenly felt the shivers from the late afternoon sunset. I felt so ill, like being very lonely and homesick. I didn't know before then *what* I was, and I resented being told. It seemed like they were wrong but I didn't know how to explain why. I didn't want to know what I was and I wanted to keep it that way.

Which I have. Whether I am posing as Chopsley, Rabid Bikini Model, for a Calvin Klein photo shoot, or exhibiting a Karen Black–designed ensemble (such as the flowing anal bead skirt), I am demonstrating that I am something in between gender, elusive and fluid.

Chopsley was a character in one of my rock videos, which was banned from television because I exposed my breasts. Assertions of female sexuality and the body usually only sneak through the mainstream if they are male-directed, as I experienced a few years ago.

We were upstate doing a Karen Black show. A Hollywood director had heard about our act and wanted us to fly out there and play ourselves as a rock band in a major motion picture, starring big stars. They did not, however, want to use the band's "real name," which I found out a little late. On the door of my trailer was a piece of masking tape that read "Pussy Juice and the Bitches from Hell." When I saw this I felt my blood curdle. I was so livid I could barely talk. Naming, inscribing myself has always been an act of self-possession. To be named by these people evoked, for me, all of the women mangled by film – I thought of the dementia of Louise Brooks or the Valium and alcohol refuge of Frances Farmer. I realized I was being used as the rent-a-wreck from New York, on a movie set where the union guys made sniffing sounds when you walked by, where they looked at you, laughed, and scratched their balls.

I decided to walk. Their sense of me as a triple-x-from-another-dimension rock pervert in a scanty costume did give me the attention I demand in my outfits, but this attention was misdirected. As a professional horror queen, I am the *subject* of my own innumerous visions of beauty, not an *object* of amusement and moronic prurience. I met with the director, Herb Ross, who wanted to "keep the laugh." He and his assistant director continued to amuse themselves by coming up with new names, whispered out of my hearing. I explained that I refused to be the brunt of a mean-spirited joke, while the elegant and tanned director of *The Turning Point* lit a Virginia Slim and tried to placate me: "Karen, Karen, sit down."

Eventually, this scene began to amuse me, pulling a prima donna shitfit and threatening to walk, like all the great screen divas before me. I chose a new name, based on a friend's super-8 film about me, and, ultimately, enjoyed watching the leading lady's face blanch as she announced, "Ladies and gentlemen . . . The Sewn Vaginas." The punk rock kids who were hired as extras snickered throughout. I liked how our low-budget notorious effort snuck into the big movie. I felt sick but good – I was participating in their laugh, laughing that they didn't understand the irony of this name. The pain and ownership signified by my own sewn vagina was emblematic of the conflict I lost and won that day.

My mother picked me up later at the L.A. Airport. It was a perfectly blue beach day. It smelled like the ocean and like cars. As we drove along the Pacific Coast Highway, my mom asked me, "Kembra, I love your band. You're so funny and I even see beyond your toplessness sometimes on stage, but what about this sewing up of your vagina?" I took a deep breath. There would be no reasonable explanation for my repossession. I just said, "Mom, I was feeling Angry. Very Angry." Maybe my answer showed her the circle that turns from humor to rage, that spins without closing; the actual horror I communicate with horror's images, camp, and conventions. That horror is female. She's never talked about it since.

Roberta Gregory

has been creating and publishing feminist comic strips since 1974. She en-

joys a fiercely loyal readership of all genders in the United States, Canada,

the United Kingdom, and Germany, where her work has appeared in

periodicals, self-published comics, collections, and anthologies.

For some years she was the only female creator to be nomi-

nated for the Eisner comic-book industry awards. Three

editions of her collected works have been pub-

lished: *A Bitch Is Born*, *As Naughty As She*

Wants to Be, and *At Work and Play With*

Bitchy Bitch. She lives in Seattle, Washington.

COMIC BOOKS
aren't just for BOYS anymore!

BY: ROBERTA GREGORY

Lotsa thanx to: TRINA ROBBINS, creator of GIRL FIGHT comix! early member of WIMMEN'S COMIX COLLECTIVE!

When I was growing up, there were always lots of comic books in the house, because my Dad wrote stories for Disney comics!

Here you GO!

Oboy!

This was back in the '50s when comic books had a bad reputation because they "corrupted" children.

WIN PRIZES!

NO... GIRLS... ALOUD?

marge's LITTLE LULU

Maybe they DID "corrupt" me...but I learned to read them REMARKABLY fast for a kid my age!

My kindergarten teacher was very impressed that I could already read...

?

WIN PRIZES UNCLE SCROOGE

...but my mother told me later that my teacher was NOT pleased when told I had learned to read by looking at "funny books"!

When I did drawings, it seemed only natural to turn them into stories and have the animals talk with word balloons.

RIDE THE PONY.

ACTUAL ART from when I was about 10 years old! →

AND, it wasn't long before I was stapling the pages together and selling these "comic books". (Mostly to Dad!)

A DOLLAR? Well... OKAY!

FUN BOOK

Usually, they'd sell for 10¢ to 25¢, but once, I got brave and charged $1.00. (It WAS a really BIG book!)

I was still reading comic books (and "real" books, too)! I still liked Uncle Scrooge and all the "Archie" books as I got older...and then I started reading Superman (and, of course, Supergirl, who had a SUPER HORSE!)

ME!

I also liked Turok and Robot Fighter, but most of the comics were all about MEN. I read some of the early Spider-Man and Silver Surfer comics, but I started getting bored with the superhero stuff.

FUN BOOK

The comic books started to print the names of artists and writers....ALL men! (Except some woman named Marie Severin.) I also liked Mad Magazine (also all by Men).

I went back to writing my OWN stories and making some of them into comics. I didn't have a lot of friends because most of the other kids had started to get "WEIRD".

Some of them acted like it was I who was "WEIRD", even though I knew better.

Later on, I decided the kids were right after all. I WAS "WEIRD" and so were my stories.

Grrrr...

Just being a girl and writing and drawing 60-page long comics was weird in itself!

I did an anti-superhero story. I did science-fiction stories. I did stories that took place in the past, and in fantasy worlds.

Most of my characters were male. Some of them were.... "homosexual" (This was WAY before "gay" was "Okay!") Some were of indeterminate gender. I didn't create many females.

I did hundreds of pages of stories and comics which I knew nobody else would ever want to read. A lot of the pages, I threw away. Some I tried to keep, but lost them many moves ago.

YUCK!

(I do have SOME stories, but, they're so... LAME I can barely READ 'em!)

Finally, I went away to college, as EVERYBODY did in 1971. Just getting out of my old environment made me feel a lot less WEIRD right away!

Gee... maybe I WON'T kill myself when I turn 20...

Life was full of adventure! Life was full of fun! People LIKED my cartoons! I did goofy little strips for the college alternative paper, Uncle Jam.

(Art for someone ELSE's story)

Late 1973 and early '74 was a pretty monumental era in my lifetime...

I was 20 years old...
I moved out of the dorms
I came out of the closet
I joined Women's Union
I discovered....
UNDERGROUND COMIX!
(better late than never.)

Just a few blocks away was a HEAD SHOP that had RACKS and RACKS of the STRANGEST comic books I'd ever SEEN...

Man, this CRUMB guy sure has a problem dealing with WOMEN...

...of course, most of them were created by MEN.

But, the STRANGEST thing was to find COMIC BOOKS that were entirely done by WOMEN!

FREAK BROTHERS
TALES OF THE LEATHER NUN
TWISTED COMICS

"AMAZONS, DYKES, LADY DETECTIVES"..?

There weren't MANY of them...but, there WERE a few... right on the racks with all the OTHER comics!

PAGE after PAGE of stories written and drawn by WOMEN! Superhero parodies! Fantasy stories! Real-life stories! Some of the women were good artists... some WEREN'T.— The stories were all DIFFERENT, but they ALL fit in.

Here's a story about a girl having to get an illegal abortion....

Here's one called: "Sandy comes out"!

WIMMEN'S COMIX

ABORTION EVE

TAINTED

You really CAN do anything in a comic book... even if.... or, maybe, ESPECIALLY if you're ___ a GIRL...

GET TA WORK!

DOINK!

CARTOON MUSE

Maybe there COULD be people who'd want to read the stories I wrote!

Women seemed to even be PUBLISHING their own comix!

"Nanny Goat Productions"...? It sounds like these two women ARE the company!

These women were funny! Irreverent! Downright... RUDE! AND, they were feminists and PROUD of it!

I started a strip in the Women's Resource Center paper called "Feminist Funnies", based on real-life (and funny) situations!

FEMINIST FUNNIES

DR. SHOVNIS, I'M GLAD YOU CHANGED YOUR MIND ABOUT LETTING ME SPEAK TO YOUR SOCIOLOGY CLASS!

(FIRST panel of the FIRST "feminist Funnies" strip!)

I sent a 4-page story to Wimmen's Comix, and they actually PUBLISHED it in issue #4! It was sort of a lesbian parody of the "Modern Romance" genre.

Don't SLACK OFF NOW..

I'M IN A COMIC BOOK!

(STILL 1974!)

I recently re-read it. It didn't seem very good. I know Wimmen's Comix had wanted more "lesbian" content, so that probably helped.

We illustrated the University Women's Resource Guide with comic strips. People kept saying "feminists have no sense of humor"...so, we'd show THEM!

Let's call it "The Ladies' Campus Companion"!

No! "LADIES", even used in a HUMOROUS way, is STILL a demeaning term!

Let me KNOW when you come up with a NAME.. *

*EVERY WOMAN CAN, if she can FIND it!

Of course, "people" still say that feminists have no sense of humor. Is this supposed to be the.... ULTIMATE INSULT, or what?

I expanded the "Feminist Funnies" strip into a whole comic book. And, I published it MYSELF, in 1976 (with a lot of helpful encouragement from Lyn Chevli and Joyce Farmer, of Nanny Goat!)

LOOK! LOOK!

Dynamite Damsels

LIBERTE EGALITE SORORITE

DYNAMITE DAMSELS

It turned out, I was the first woman to solo-publish and to distribute a real regulation-sized comic book.

LOOK OUT, world!

CRAPPY HAIR-CUT

REAL shirt!

SUPER DYKE

This was 1976, and women were beginning to start their own RECORD COMPANIES, too!

Underground Comix didn't last very long after 1976. Obscenity laws hounded the publishers. Printing costs went up. Head Shops were closed down by paraphernalia laws.

POKE-POKE

CARTOON MUSE

I had a few more stories published by Wimmens Comix and Nanny Goat. Throughout the '80s, I drew HUNDREDS of pages in semi-obscurity, though I was in almost every issue of Gay Comix.

It's been more than 20 years since I first got published, and comix are STILL the major focus of my life. I've been doing a LOT of work, and Bitchy Bitch has helped to make my comics a BIT better known, but STILL way obscure when you think about "POP" culture.

KEEP DRAWING!

1995 was the FIRST year I made a (VERY meagre!) living JUST from my comics! Twenty years ago, I never would've thought it REMOTELY possible!

VERY few alternative comix creators - men OR women - manage to quit their "day job"... MAYBE someday that'll CHANGE!

REAL alternative comix, 1995!

GIRL HERO

REAL GIRL

GIRL TALK

ACTION GIRL

In 1995, it actually began to seem that Comic Books might be for... GIRLS! FIND a good comic book shop and SUPPORT comix by WOMEN!

Marge Piercy

is the author of twelve collections of poetry including *The Moon Is Always Female*, *Circles on the Water*, *My Mother's Body*, *Available Light*, and *Mars and Her Children*. She has also written twelve novels including *Women on the Edge of Time*, *Braided Lives*, *Gone to Soldiers*, *Summer People*, *He, She & It* (which won the Arthur C. Clarke Award for Best Science Fiction), and *The Longings of Women*. Based in Wellfleet, Massachusetts, she is the poetry editor of *Tikkun*.

a dissatisfaction without a name

a dissatisfaction without a name

marge piercy

WHEN did I first become a feminist? I suspect it was around puberty, when I began to think hard about what I saw in my family and around me.

My mother had been sent to work as a chambermaid when she was still in the tenth grade, because her family was large and poor and needed the income she could bring in. She had an active mind, a strong sense of politics, and an immense curiosity. She read a great deal, haphazardly. Because she had no framework of knowledge of history or of the world in which to fit what she read or what she experienced, intelligent observations jostled with superstitions and folk beliefs. She was a mental magpie, gathering up and carrying off to mull over anything that attracted her attention, anything bright, anything shiny, anything that glittered out of the ordinary boredom of being a housewife. There was, truly, something birdlike about her, a tiny woman (only four-foot-ten) with glossy black hair who would cock her head to the side and stare with bright dark eyes.

She had grown up in a radical Jewish family where politics was discussed and debated. She had a sense of class conflict and social reality that was the most consistent and logical part of her mind. My father could easily be seduced by racism, sexism, Republican promises of lowering taxes. Like many working-class men of his time, he started out on the left and moved steadily toward the right. My mother never wavered in her analysis of who was on her side and who was not. She trusted few politicians, but she appreciated those who she thought fought for the rights of ordinary people.

My father very much enjoyed sexist jokes and told them till the end of his life, ignoring my attitudes if I was present. They were a way of knocking on the wooden reality of how things were with men and women and showing how sound it was. My mother did not tell such jokes and seldom laughed at them. However, she had attitudes of her own. She admired women who fought for other women, but she also had contempt for women. She complained of women's weakness, at the same time that she herself had few strengths to fall back on. She viewed sex as a powerful force that carried off women into servitude. A woman's sexuality was a deity of tremendous energy who exacted a lifelong price from her.

When I was little, I thought of my mother as very strong – for certainly she had power over me. My father would punish me, severely, with fists and feet and with a wooden yardstick. But my mother was usually the one who set the rules for me, since my father did not take much interest, except sometimes to decide I must do something I didn't want to do, because he despised cowards: climb something, cross a narrow high bridge, whatever. These demands had little to do with me but were part of a war between the two of them. She had many fears (he was driving too fast, too dangerously) that in some way pleased him. Her fear proved he was strong and able, in comparison with my mother (whom he never taught to drive). But I was the battleground in which he demonstrated how women were afraid by demanding I do things I feared.

So I learned to do them. I learned to overcome my fear and do foolhardy things, never without thinking but without giving an outward sign of my fear. I did it partly in a futile effort to gain his respect, which could never be granted to me. That respect was never attainable because of my sex and because my mother and I were Jewish, and he was not. He was not anything in particular. He thought of himself as English, Anglo-Saxon, but he was only one-quarter English; he was half Welsh and one-quarter Scottish. He was far more a Celt than an Anglo-Saxon. He was a moody man who feared and denied emotions; they were what he truly regarded as sins. He liked to drink; he liked to eat what he regarded as proper masculine food (meat and potatoes mostly); he liked to play poker and other mild betting games. But he intensely disliked being aware he felt anything except anger. His anger was swift and thunderous. He never hit my mother but he frightened her. Again, I was the surrogate. He could and did hit me. Also my older brother.

My mother had a temper of her own. She got angry as quickly as he did. She had a far more vivid vocabulary of curses, some in Yiddish (used only with me), most in English. *Shit and molasses!* she would yell. *Piss blood and drink it!* Her temper was released on me, of course, and on objects. I remember her at the kitchen table pulling the cloth laden with supper – dishes and food and flowers – and throwing it against the wall. She broke dishes with abandon. Never the good dishes. No, she broke the dishes they got as giveaways at the movies or bought secondhand at garage and yard sales.

She was not a middle-class lady. She cursed, she thought of herself as fastidious but wasn't, she lost her temper, she liked bright colors and gaudy objects. She was overtly sexual. She was immensely curious and loved plants and animals. She was always hungry for conversation, for communication, for something of interest. My early and middle childhood centered on her. My father was dangerous but peripheral. When I was young, I could not understand why she never seemed to get what she wanted.

I remember a particular birthday of hers, which came in November, the year I turned thirteen. My mother always fussed about presents. She would shop carefully for my father, sometimes buying his gift several months in advance. She liked to give presents and she desperately enjoyed being given them. I always gave her as nice a present as I could afford. That went on until she died at eighty-seven (we think). I still have many of them.

For her birthday, my father gave her a new garbage can for the kitchen and a broom. She wept for hours. There was not only boredom in the gift but insult. I brooded over this: Wherein lay the insult? I said to her, "Why don't you buy yourself what you want? Why does he have to give it to you? Why don't you go out and buy yourself a good red dress, a new coat, a leather purse?" She looked at me as if I was crazy and said, "He'd never put up with me spending that kind of money on myself."

"What business is it of his what you spend money on?"

Again she glared at me, an idiot child. "*It isn't my money.*"

I began then to understand why my mother finally had to defer to my father, why my mother could yell and sulk and wheedle and brood, but could never win. She worked all the time, obviously, but the only money she had was what he gave her for the house. They quarreled constantly about how much she spent on groceries. Everything was controlled by him. He bought himself a new car every two or three years, but there was no money for me to go to the dentist. My teeth rotted in my mouth and broke off. It wasn't until I was putting myself through college that I spent my first semester mostly sitting in the dental school having my teeth fixed by student dentists. He owned every power tool he saw advertised. I went off to college without a winter coat. My mother developed cataracts but never saw an eye doctor. At eighty-seven, she was still cleaning the house without help.

When I was fifteen, we moved to a bigger house in Detroit, where she began to rent out rooms. Now she had money of her own, finally, which she could use as she pleased. But it was too late. She said to me, "I can't leave him now. The house is in his name. I'd starve."

When my mother was eighty-six, she demanded that we drive down to visit her in Florida, where my parents then lived. She had a present to give me that was too big to be carried back on the plane. She did give me a box of silverplate that would easily have fit in a suitcase, but what she really wanted to give me waited until my father left the house. Then from hiding places all over their tiny home she pulled out single dollar bills, one after the other. For an hour she piled up dollar bills, until she had given me over $1,200, stuffed in cracks in the floor, hidden in closets, thrust into coat pockets, under dresser scarves, in the bottom of dry vases. This was her gift, an immense bequest. She had saved it out of grocery money, squirreling it away. She knew she was going to die soon (she had had a stroke she had told no one about and soon would have another that would kill her), and she wanted to leave me an inheritance. It had taken her enormous effort to save and secrete these bills.

It became clear to me sometime between the ages of thirteen and fifteen that economics was the bedrock on which any independence had to be built. If I couldn't make a living, I would be as wretched as my mother. If I depended on a man to support me, I would be enslaved. It was that simple to me.

In contrast to my mother was my Aunt Ruth, who was midway between us in age. She worked. She had only a high school diploma, which kept her from advancing in the navy, kept her from advancing up any corporate ladder. But she was bright and ambitious and she made a living. She took up bowling and won trophies. She was one of the few women jocks I knew. When she married and moved into a middle-class suburb, she took up golf instead, and soon she was filling the house with golf trophies. She was a far more observant Jew than my mother, but she was also more worldly. She dressed like a working woman. She had no children and she spent her money as she pleased, even after she married.

Her husband began to beat and abuse her. She had my grandmother living with her most of the year (every summer she came to us). That complicated Ruth's choices. My mother said, "Poor Ruth! What can she do?" But Ruth cut through it all and ran off with another man who was much kinder to her and with whom she lived the rest of her life. She eloped, taking my grandmother with her. It was clear to me that if you earned your own money and you had the guts to do what you wanted, you would never be stuck – as my own mother was.

I went through childhood and adolescence brooding a great deal about the war between women and men, about the inequalities I saw and did not want in my own life. I had no word for my concerns, no political framework in which to think about what I observed and what I worried about. For the next ten years, whenever I was involved with a man, I would eventually feel an enormous weight of despair. Both men and women told me that was how things were, unequal, and that I should accept the female situation with graceful acquiescence because it had always been so and would always be so: this was the message of high and low culture, from the novels and poetry we read to the messages of advertisements and men's and women's glossy and pulp magazines, the movies we went to, and the songs played over the radio. Everything said men are strong and women are weak, and women like it that way. Men rule and women are ruled, and women like it that way. Men earn money and women stay home and have babies and raise children (and then what?) and spend money. Men think; women feel. Men plan; women flirt. Men do; women are done. Anything else was unnatural, and what could be worse than an unnatural woman?

By my last two years of college, I was a better writer than the men around me in writing classes and in the school journals. I had begun to win prizes. Prizes were, after all, won under sexless pseudonyms. Yet I never received the respect accorded the men my age. I could not understand why I should not be taken seriously. I had no more affairs than many of the men in my circles, yet my few affairs were scandalous. I was a scarlet woman, a shameless hussy.

Similarly, I had no name for the invisibility that came over me when I married, left graduate school, and began to work as a secretary to support my husband's graduate studies in physics. I was aware I had suddenly become invisible, inaudible, of no account. I spent a long time figuring that one out.

Then suddenly Simone de Beauvoir put it all in focus and gave me a name for my discontent. At twenty-two, I read *The Second Sex*. That amazing book provided the impetus to walk out of my marriage and rethink the choices I had made. I had a vocabulary with which I could define and retain insights that had come to me over the years, but which society had labeled crazy. I was not crazy, after all. Now I knew what I was: I was a feminist.

a name

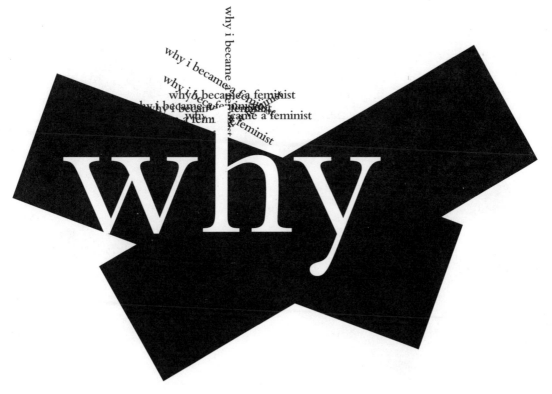

I became a feminist

Incest is still not a verb

in the English language

Lillian Allen

is a poet, playwright, and filmmaker whose writings and recordings have won international recognition. One of the birth mothers of dub poetry, she has produced two Juno Award–winning recordings of poetry with music for adult audiences, and she has also recorded and written works for young people. Her most recent published collection of poetry is *Women Do This Every Day*. She teaches creative writing at the Ontario College of Art and Design, in Toronto.

My nephew can tell you the moment he felt "humanism" failed him. It happened when his dad took him fishing, wanting to get their male bonding thing under way. When the first fish was hooked and caught, his dad (my brother) held it with a gloved hand to unhook it from its bait.

The young boy reached toward his father imploring: "That hurts, Daddy . . . you're hurting the fish." As the fish flipped and flapped for its life, my nephew saw images of baby Flipper on the rocks before him. "Put that fish back, Daddy, put him back. He doesn't like not being in his house."

The end of the story as it travels in family circles is that my nephew refused to eat any of the fish for dinner, and has never eaten animal, bird, or fish since.

There are several moments and events in my life that have had a profound effect on transforming my consciousness into a feminist one. But the event that made this evolution categorical and irretreatable – the one that stands out most in my mind – is the story of a young girl named Nellie.

There was a saying that rough boys bragged of on street corners and respectable men nudged each other with in private conversations. It goes like this: "Sperms don't have flashlights," meaning that sperms have no way of seeing in the dark and therefore were not responsible for where they landed. That many young Jamaican girls were the brunt of this "joke" is a tragedy that is well documented and too often still occurring.

When I was growing up in Spanish Town, Jamaica, periodically you would see young girls who would start to swell up and become drawn. Before long, they would disappear from the neighborhood. Some would come back after months or years, some would never return. They were all types: robust, rosy, ripe, vinelike, introverted, quiet, loud, the swan, the duckling. Some innocent, some not. The only thing they had in common was that they were girls.

The thirteen-year-old Nellie reincarnated in my poem "Nellie Belly Swelly" was one of those young girls of my youth who didn't have a chance. The hand that fed her, put a roof over her head, disciplined her, instilled the love of God in her, showed her affection, drove fear of failure into her, was the one who raped, impregnated, and incested her. The word *incest* is still not a verb in the English language. Instead, *incest* is used as a euphemism for rape because it's a "family matter." The word *incest* as a noun – a person, place, or thing – allows a distancing of the perpetrator from the crime. *Incestrape* twinned, as a single verb, would be a more fitting description for this "family matter."

Nellie was the kid with the funny squeaky laugh; a bird's pitch. She was as frivolous as she was cuddly. By all pronunciations in the neighborhood, she was a spoilt pick'ny. Little Nellie hung around with my sisters and me; she was one of us.

Nellie lived with her mother, a hardworking, nurturing woman, who tended to church matters with impeccable grace. A former "A" level scholar, she got pregnant before she could go to college, was turfed out of her home, and was disowned by her family because of it. No father appeared on the scene. Being "used goods" she considered herself among the fortunate when an ambitious teacher nineteen years her elder returned from England and wanted to marry her. He was the "man of the house" that was needed for the "proper" upbringing of the child, to keep her on the straight and narrow path. And so he did: little Nellie's new father was dictatorial, strict, and known to vigorously practice corporal punishment on Nellie and on his students at school. He was highly regarded for this.

It is not easy to forget the Easter that I sensed a change in Nellie, like she had become a different person; the laughter and lightness went out of her. She became withdrawn and swollen and always sad and forlorn. It wasn't long after that she disappeared from the neighborhood and from our light-hearted frolics and childhood meanderings.

Months later, Nellie returned, oddly womanish and much older than her years. We were never allowed to play with her, and any questioning would bring some "licks" or other severe disciplining from our parents. The talk around Nellie was always ominous, always in whispers like some evil lurking, ready to be unleashed as we spoke.

Nellie had become a shadow. She was thrust into a seemingly endless routine of near slavery – cooking, cleaning house and yard, laundering, ironing, and being loaned out to cook and clean for other people. She played no more as children do. Every now and then we would catch a glimpse of her as she leaned on a broom in her yard, staring into deep space as if she were seeking a secret door to fall through and float away. Or sometimes at night, for a brief fifteen or so minutes she would sit freshened by a bath and clean clothes at a window facing the street. That was all we ever got to see of Nellie for the next two years until word reached us of a turn in her fortunes. Nellie was going to emigrate to New York, to the Nirvana of our childhood imagination. I celebrated silently for her because, whatever it was, I was sure that her redemption had come – at last.

I didn't think of Nellie much after that. When we were out playing we would watch the planes fly over and send with it lots of good wishes for Nellie. When we saw anyone from America, whether from Connecticut or California, we would ask after Nellie. And although they had never heard of her, we would send hellos anyway, just in case. But secretly in our hearts, we wished that Nellie was getting funky, eating lots of ice cream and pizza, wearing mink, and driving a Cadillac.

It was several years later that I too went to live in New York City. One Saturday night, I attended a hometown party in the Bronxwood section of the Bronx. There, across the room, amidst heavy reggae rhythms, my eyes and Nellie's caught each other's. She was perfect. And cuddly again. Her youth had returned to the curvature of her smile. I could sense the high-pitched breathless laughter radiating from her body before I could hear it. We met halfway across the room and looked at each other. Nellie beamed. The questions I'd wanted to ask for six years rolled out of my mouth, tumbling uncontrollably:

"What did you do?" I asked.

"Heh, heh. Nor even a hello or nuttin?" She embraced me.

"What happened . . . What did you do?"

Nellie looked at me. She knew what I sought. She smiled. She had herself back, I could see.

"I had a baby . . . ," she said.

"No shit." I stopped myself.

"No shit . . . ," she echoed with a tone that had lost its childhood frivolity and hesitancy – a full-bodied person behind the voice.

And the conversation went on. I discovered that Nellie had gotten pregnant not by any of the fourteen-, fifteen-, or sixteen-year-old boys that were around us when we were growing up but by her stepfather, the schoolteacher, the guy who had since become vice-principal, the guy who meted out the strictest discipline and was a symbol of moral rightness in the community.

As my nephew could point to the precise moment that propelled him into a life of vegetarianism, I recall my meeting with Nellie at the party in the Bronx as one of the most profound events of my life.

What separated me, my sisters, and other little girls like us from Nellie was maybe a street, or a different mother, or a different father. Maybe a different country, a different culture, a different class, a different social status. But since none of these are our choosing, the all too prevalent tragedy of child abuse and incest could have happened to any of us. Finding your way out of ignorance is easier and infinitely more wholesome than constantly looking away. Ignorance is not bliss. Not unlike the jokes of rough boys on the street corner where I grew up, it is a way of denying responsibility and complicity. Ignorance is an expensive privilege for all those who choose to exercise it. In the case of incest and child abuse, children are paying with their childhoods, with their bodies, with their little hearts, with their minds. Some with their lives every day.

The unspoken, almost universal traditions of community and family values of protective silence are complicit in these terrible tragedies of young girl lives. Our individual silence not only allows such grave injustices to continue but also serves to retroactively justify them.

At seventeen, not being "political" and not knowing shit, I knew one thing for sure – then and there in the beat of that pouncing reggae party, in the rising blue mists of marijuana smoke and a feverish sense of excitement of a generation coming into its own, I had to take the side of my friend Nellie. I had to become part of the solution. I had to do it for myself, for all the women and young girls and for the world to become a safer, saner, and better place. That is how I became a feminist.

Nellie Belly Swelly

Nellie was thirteen
don't care bout no fellow
growing in the garden
among the wild flowers

she Mumma she dig & she plant
nurtures her sod
tends the rose bush
in the garden pod

lust leap the garden fence
pluck the rose bud
bruk it ina the stem

oh no please no
was no self defense
oh no please no
without pretense
offered no defense
to a little little girl
called Nellie

Nellie couldn't understand
Mr. Thompson's hood
so harsh, so wrong
in such an offensive

Nellie plead, Nellie beg
Nellie plead, Nellie beg

but Mr. Thompson's hood
went right through her legs

knowing eyes blamed her

Nellie disappeared from sight
news spread wide
the months went by
psst psst psst Nellie belly swelly
Nellie belly swelly Nellie belly swelly

children skipped to Nellie's shame

Nellie returned from the night
gave up her dolls
and the rose bush died
Nellie Momma cried Nellie Momma cried
little Nellie no more child again

No sentence was passed
on this menacing ass
who plundered Nellie's childhood

In her little tiny heart
Nellie understood war

She mustered an army within her
strengthened her defense
and mined the garden fence
No band made a roll
skies didn't part
for this new dawn
in fact, nothing herald it
when this feminist was born

Nellie

Twosome

Sonja Ahlers

is an artist based in Victoria, British Columbia, whose work has been reviewed in *Exclaim* magazine. Her window-display art has inspired several exhibitions of her two-dimensional collages and box and medicine-chest installations. She is forming a band called Kiki Bridges. She and the artist Chantale recently co-exhibited their work in Victoria.

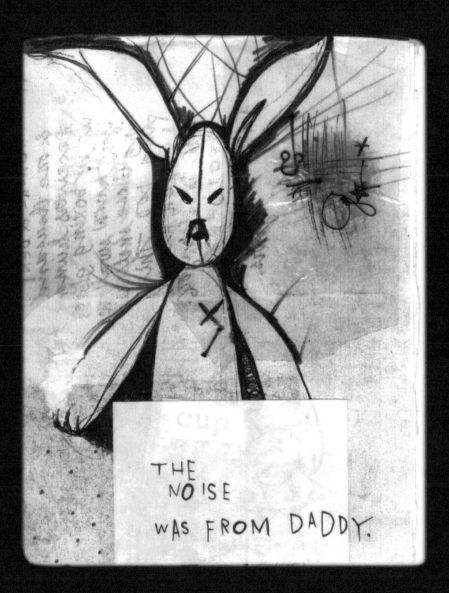

I'm gonna burn the letters
I'm gonna burn the letters
letters I wrote when I was high

this ~~heart~~ is broken bleeding &
TOUGH ENOUGH .   & sacred

pulls hard

on the cigarette.

back w/ three or four
                sugars.

     you drink coffee ?

he is through   oh yah
     stomping around
          my head.

MARSHMALLOW FLUFF

I'm gonna burn those letters
they mean nothing now.

they mean nothing now.

Q: what's the matter

Hey ↗

↘

?

A: oh - nothing.

Baby Hermes

lye,aspirin & ether
Me & you

& the space between.
Milk white skinny bones
do make me sick
bleached bone I will crush
myself to powder toot I will
breathe & push out as far as far

away the moon is which you did not
not hang
& after that you will be gone
I'll grow huge & weightless
I'll eat fat chocolate hearts
& I'll float away

a curling iron in my hands
a dangling ~~cords~~ & participles *like*
                    chords
Pure light.

You WIll Never reach Me.

choke choking on chicken bones
& boring **BORE** rights in
me & guitars &
FEATHERS & FATHERS
EVERYWHERE & ALL OVER
of course
RECOURSE
& PAINSTAKING
& ~~I some fucking~~
pains ~~I took~~

extremities
extremities
THE
BURN-
ING

in the queen - SIZED
on the queen -sized bed
BED
MATTRESS IS
DISTRESS

& take
away & took
from the kingsize
subtract the
queen -sized bed
KING SIZED

FARAH FAWCETT

& make it
one. make it
singled - out.
single burn the bed
that's it (handedly)

polish.

I wanted to be small
so I curled up/into
a ball

That's all. That's all.

FLY ME
ON THE
WING

There' Is this girl somewhere
There's this girl nowhere
up in the sky
she's laying guilt trips
like a pro carpet layer/
liar & taking away my
quilt just makes me
rotten & cold
pepsin & hydro chloric acid
churns & burns in the
pit of my stomach
besides. I'm peeling
myself off of the CEILING

Break & Breaking
till all the way
broken
& entering
& not much forgiveness
here. NO. NOT much @ all.

so
I get rid of
what breaks me

down like rock salt
on black ice.

That's it.
I'm moving to Spain
thats it - 'cause I'm taking pains

I've never ~~been~~ there before

I don't even know —
I just ~~know I~~ WANNA GO.

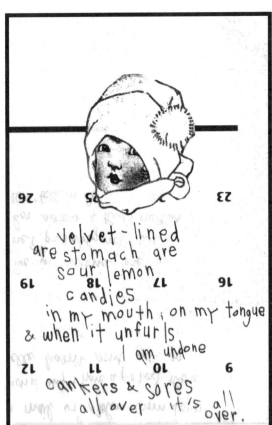

velvet - lined
are stomach are
sour lemon
candies
in my mouth; on my tongue
& when it unfurls
I am undone
cankers & sores
all over it's all over.

This ageing
this careless~~x~~ness is uselessness
this carelessness is next to useless
                                    ness.

some shit aboutCatholisism
some shit about Cathechism

these are orange baby aspirins that
the girls ate like candy
& daddy lopped off my blue bunny's ears
& I in turn lopped off my own ear lobes

& my solar plexus ~~is~~ is in the wrong
place & my head space is in the sunken
living ~~room~~ room
   because only the living rooms die.
There is no rheumatism
no not here.

A crying guitar is sounding like my
baby cat
& I'd~~f~~ say
the span of my discontent stretches
   ~~wingtip~~ wingtip to wingtip

      last night i know

      I know
      the moon ate too much

   as in sanguinary
   as in hemic

so when you're in the shower,
baby
I'm gonna flush the toilet.

paper
ghost

I don't know about you
but
~~t~~hat's what I'm gonna do.

Don't think, honey. Just throw.

i was excommunicated
because sometimes the pope
tells me no hope no hope no hope
knotted silk is tied tight
around his neck pearls between the tiny
knots late later is the iceskater
on thin, thin ice

xxxx hangging rope is hanging five

He told me
he doesn't like to use soap

just dumb girls xxxx like me.

oh, it is okay. oh, it doesn't matter.
i don't know her anymore
i excommunicated her

So

  after I crazy-glued my fingertips
to my eyelids
I fixated myself on one paragraph
  ƒx for hours & hours
    & between the letters i began to see
    a slight wisp of a girl with a truck
                              driver's mouth.
    then I undid my own belly button
    just to see what would happen
    cause my dad took my brother to the
      laundermat to WASH

  wash his brain again again
  & me -
  well, Ismashed my head up into a wall
  I
  like I'll drink this tea & smash my
  cup, too.

  breaking things makes me feel better
  so you see
  I am into destruction
  which is reason enough
  which is reason enough
  for a daughter

It Was A Drunk X Thing

baby - need a lift?

NO.

キャンデー

品 名

don't psychoanalyze the cat.
my dad told me that once.

an ALL-TIME LOW.

new pillow

another new pillow

HEY BABY—WHERE YOU GOING?

A Hatred for the
Hotrod.

Just get over it
de-frocked & see
this hand grenade
pull its key
& you'll have found
                    me
breaking my own jaw
in a last-ditch
attempt to
                THIS
lock kick down/door
shut.

WIPE
DOWN
& CLEAN

YOUR
FEELERS

PLEASE PLEASE PLEASE

I needed those clipped wings
& that's a lie times a thousand
clipped wings & all that & your
love by the outfield
silver sliver moon
& I could hardly see it.

MARJORIE INGALL

is a former senior writer for *Sassy* magazine. She now writes for *Ms.*, *Mademoiselle*, *The Web*, and numerous other magazines, CD-ROMS, and Web sites. Her book *The Field Guide to North American Males* was published in 1997. She lives in San Francisco.

MARJORIE INGALL

WHY

MR. LEVEQUE SUCKED

1. What Mr. Leveque Looked Like

On any given day in 1983, Mr. Leveque was likely to be wearing a cardigan with the sleeves rolled up and baggy faded jeans, to be down with the hipster youth of Grade Ten Advanced English. Mr. Leveque did the comb-over, so each glistening hair-stripe stood out upon his shiny pink skull. He always had five-o'clock shadow, even if you had English at eleven a.m. He had jowls, hooded eyes, and fat fingers. The backs of his pale hands were covered with gleaming black hairs.

2. What I Looked Like

On any given day in 1983, I was likely to be wearing an armful of black rubber bracelets, a long white vintage cotton slip, and a Rhode Island Public Transit Authority bus token on a black rubber cord around my neck. I thought this looked very cool. I usually wore one pink high-top and one turquoise high-top. For symmetry, one eye was heavily lined in blue eyeliner, the other in purple eyeliner.

3. What Mr. Leveque's Classroom Looked Like

Over the blackboard in Mr. Leveque's classroom was a big sign, a ribbon of yellowed, dot-matrix-spittled computer paper reading "Abandon Hope All Ye Who Enter Here."

4. How We Whiled Away the Academic Hours

Mr. Leveque could teach whatever he wanted because we were Advanced. Thus we read *Kon-Tiki: Across the Pacific by Raft* and *The Sand Pebbles*. (I think maybe Mr. Leveque served in the navy. Or could be he just enjoyed the ocean.) We were psyched that we got to spend three classes zoning out watching super-tan Steve McQueen in *The Sand Pebbles* on video while the less advanced English classes had to read *David Copperfield* and *Romeo and Juliet*.

Unfortunately, poetry was nastier. Mr. Leveque made us memorize the birth dates, death dates, places of birth, places of death, alma maters, and wives' names of thirteen American poets. It did not occur to any of us to protest. Such arbitrary nyah-nyah was par for high school. When the morning of the test rolled around, I agonized for about a minute, then carefully wrote all the dates on the surgical tape wrapping my finger, which sported a splint from volleyball team (Johnetta's serve was lethal).

Today I can tell you that either Carl Sandburg or Robert Frost died in 1963.

When we reached Whitman, Mr. Leveque pranced up and down the room shrieking "Little Wally Whitman!" He swung his hips and held his arm out in front of him, hairy hand dangling at the wrist. The boys bellowed with laughter. Mr. Leveque said sneeringly that Whitman stood naked on the beach and screamed his poems to the ocean. Everyone knew what *that* meant.

5. What I Did Whenever Mr. Leveque Did His Whitman Impression

A. Felt bad for not defending Whitman even though I didn't know any fags then. I *felt* physically sick every time Mr. Leveque started sashaying, even as the corners of my mouth moved upward in a simpering smile of Grade Ten Stepford agreeability. I knew Whitman was a better poet, that "Song of Myself" sure as shit trumped John Greenleaf Whittier's clunky sincere verse about foliage. But I sat and smiled. **B.** Obsessed over the morality of writing birth dates and death dates on my splint. But I did it anyway.

When we got to the part of the curriculum where we studied vocab, Mr. Leveque wrote a series of essays containing many huge words cobbled together from Greek and Latin roots, which we had to rewrite in conversational English. Mr. Leveque liked this method because it meant that even though it was vocabulary, he could grade us subjectively; you weren't only being graded on whether you could figure out what the big words meant, you were being graded on how much he liked your paragraph.

Adding to the challenge was the fact that sometimes Mr. Leveque's big words didn't mean what the dictionary said. Like, in Advanced U.S. History we learned that *manumission* meant "freeing the slaves." He told us it meant "hitting someone." *Manu-* meant "hand." *Mission* meant "sending out." Ergo, hitting someone. Anyone who tried to reason out how the essay could be about freeing the slaves got a C plus or lower. When I told my mom she had a shitfit, but I just shook my head at her naïveté. If she called the principal, I informed her, I'd kill her.

6. How Mr. Leveque Graded

Either Jared Star or Mark Robbins or both Jared Star *and* Mark Robbins got As. A bunch of girls got A minuses. Bs and Cs were strewn among the remaining boys and girls in an egalitarian manner. The girls all joked about it and pretended to fume over the injustice of possessing that lame-ass A-blocking extra X chromosome, but it wasn't like it mattered. Actually it was a relief. In most classes it was a struggle to maintain the coveted A minus, high enough so that everyone knew you were smart but not so high that you were a loser geek suckup nimrod.

7. What Mr. Leveque Did to the Girls

Walked up and down the rows of desks, and our shoulders would stiffen if he paused behind us because sooner or later he would stop and rub someone's shoulders in a circle around and around and around. Then he would walk some more.

To complain about this would be unfathomable. It would be like trying to stop miosis. Mitosis. Whatever.

8. What Happened in Real Life

Real life happened outside of classrooms. People did whatever. Talked, wrote bad Gothic poetry, dribbled soccer balls, drew hearts on their knees where the jeans were ripped, played bass in garage bands. I was not a Writer then (i.e., not a member of the literary magazine or *The Caduceus*), but in real life I wrote an essay that actually mattered to me, something different from the worker-drone dutiful light-and-dark-imagery-in-*The-Scarlet-Letter* essays I wrote in class.

Back then, I used to have post-nuclear nightmares, the full-on cliché. Buildings standing as if made of Pixy Stix, hollow and pastel-colored, everything silent and unpeopled. I wrote about my dreams for this anti-nuke group I was active in, and I won a statewide essay contest. I'd never won anything before, and I was beyond psyched. In my moment of literary triumph, I decided to bring real life into the classroom and actually tell Mr. Leveque. I did not explicitly know what I wished to accomplish by this.

9. What I Said to Mr. Leveque

"So, um, what I was wondering was how to do better in your class? It's been really bothering me? Because I try my hardest. And I've never gotten less than an A before this year. And I just won this essay contest, and so I'm thinking maybe I'm not such a bad writer, and maybe you want to read it?"

10. What Mr. Leveque Said to Me

"Margie, do you know anything about cars? Well, some cars have two-cylinder engines, and some cars have six-cylinder engines. You are a two-cylinder engine, and Jared Star is a six-cylinder engine. You can never be a six-cylinder engine, but you can be the best damn two-cylinder engine you can be. It's nice that you won an essay contest, but tell me one thing: Did Jared Star enter? Well, now you see why you won."

11. How My Worldview was Irrevocably Changed by This Earth-Shattering Moment

I said, "Um, okay." And left. And retched into the third-floor girls' room toilet.

Suddenly I recognized the scenario I'd been hoping for: Mr. Leveque would be pinned like a bug by the impossibly sparkly, withering things I would say, and he would know I saw through his little-man-behind-the-curtain charade. He would know the clueless pathetic error of his ways with such clarity ("Why, Marjorie is brilliant! Jared Star is an inferior, pretentious boy moron! I must kill myself right now!") that everything would be different from then on.

Nothing was different. Actually, that isn't quite true. I changed; I stopped buying in. It was quite liberating, in a way. Hey, I'd *tried* to challenge the bubble-world of high school injustice, and it was bigger than I was, and that freed me. I started to see myself as an unbalanced atom, a negatively charged little ion. I got publicly funny, snide and unpredictable. In my last two years of high school, I cared less if people thought I was smart, and I cared less if teachers thought I was insolent. Knowing that no girl was *ever* going to be a six-cylinder engine in certain classrooms forced my hand. It's like this study I read about that said African-American girls usually have better body images than white girls, perhaps because they've recognized that their beauty isn't going to be appreciated by the dominant culture anyway. Maybe they learn to trust their internal voices more. Maybe that's what I did too.

12. What Might Constitute a Happy Ending

A. Mr. Leveque saved me from remaining a Good Girl who always waits to be called on, sits with her knees together, and gets blindsided by American Association of University Women reports about how dicked over she is by the educational process. **B.** In *Kon-Tiki* they get off the fucking raft. I guess you get out of high school. That's something.

36

strokes

TRISH THOMAS

Trish Thomas's

USED TO THINK it was my civic duty to be the best cock-sucker in the whole world. I used to be married to a man. I used to watch *Wide World of Sports*, read *TV Guide* magazine, drink Schlitz Malt Liquor tallboys, and smoke fat joints. I used to put on full makeup, including foundation, to go to the corner store to pick up a six-pack. My children used to live with me.

That's pretty much it for the formative years. A few things stand out.

At twenty-three, I read a grocery store paperback of *The Women's Room* and put my maiden name back on my driver's license. You're splitting up the family, Richard said when he saw it. A couple of years later my Aunt Helen died and left me twenty-five grand.

work has been published in *Bad Attitude, Fireweed, Frighten the Horses, Los Angeles Reader, Mondo 2000, New Orleans City Business, Quim, San Francisco Weekly, Taste of Latex,* and *Wicked Women,* and in the anthologies *Best American Erotica 1993, The Girl Wants To,* and *A Movement of Eros.* She currently resides in New Orleans. She has finally hugged her grandchildren and has started wearing dresses again. Trish Thomas is at work on a collection of personal essays about men, women, romance, writing, and regional personalities.

Maybe I'll go to college, I thought, but Richard said, You should use it for the family, so I bought us a couch, a color TV, a kitchen table and chairs, a used powder-blue Monte Carlo, a two-bedroom house, and Viacom's full cable package. One morning I got fumbled awake from behind for the last time and slammed a leftover glass of red wine against the bedroom wall. I took to sleeping on the couch. I accidentally watched a late late movie that showed two women making love on a massage table. I got restless. I went out drinking with Sandy. I met Kevin. We spent the night kissing on the grass by the Echo Park lake. I thought, This is living.

I went back home and told Richard I didn't want to be married any more. He split and took the kids with him. (The next time I saw them they were teenagers.) Kevin came right over, sat down at the kitchen table, and cried. I'd never seen a man cry before and I was moved, even after it became clear that he was crying not for me and my unfortunate situation but for himself, because he'd been kicked out of his apartment. Don't worry, I said, you can stay with me, but he didn't want to live there, in that house, where I'd lived with my husband (what if he came back?), so I packed up my clothes and moved to an apartment in Glendale. I called the kids in Montgomery. Did you bring our toys? they wanted to know. Christ. I didn't even sell the house.

One night Kevin didn't show and I tossed all his stuff in the Dumpster. The next day he called and we made up. Later that week he busted my lip for the first time. I thought, I'm a woman now. He moved in more stuff. He told a girl at the On Klub that he liked her butt so I took the new batch of stuff to his buddy's house in Burbank, piled it on the front steps, rang the doorbell, and drove off in a huff. Kevin called and we made up again. After that it got monotonous. Eventually we got kicked out of the apartment in Glendale for making too much noise. I found us a place in Hollywood. We ate acid, black beauties, pink hearts, Christmas trees, and Percodans, smoked hash, pot, and opium, drank Myer's rum and orange juice, and snorted heroin. I got slapped, kicked, knocked down, my ear split open. Kevin drove me to the hospital for stitches himself. The next day I called in sick, pretending I'd been mugged. I'd like to say I kicked him out after that but the truth is he left "to get some space." Nobody likes a wussie.

I turned twenty-seven, got pregnant from a one-night stand, had an abortion, kissed Sandy, got my tubes tied, started smoking cigarettes, fell in love with my first faggot, slept with two girls, read *Rubyfruit Jungle*, decided everyone was bisexual, moved north to San Francisco, and enrolled at City College.

I turned twenty-eight. I went to an all-girl party and met a bona fide bulldagger who showed me how to have an orgasm *during* sex. I decided I was a dyke. I bought a leather jacket and stopped waxing my legs. She rode me to the bars on the back of her motorcycle. She knew everybody and everybody knew her. I thought, I wish *I* had a history.

I read *Woman Hating* by Andrea Dworkin and found out all women everywhere are doomed for life. I met a college girl who told me if my father painted houses for a living then I was lower-class, like her, and that was how the world saw me, and that was how the world would always see me. This news gave me, like the aspiring rock star in *This Is Spinal Tap* upon visiting Elvis Presley's grave, "a bit too *much* fucking perspective."

I dumped the bulldagger and let the college girl move in. Right away I found out if you ask somebody to wash her dishes once in a while, you're throwing an "elitist trip." Then we had to stop having sex because once back in junior high school some dude had tried to touch her tits, leaving her with "issues," which were now, unfortunately, "up." We could still be girlfriends, though, we'd just be "non-monogamous." What's that? I had to ask. Where I came from, people had regular relationships and pretended nobody was cheating. Lesbians, it turns out, have superior relationships and pretend nobody's getting hurt.

I slept with a few girls and she threw a few tantrums – not because I was sleeping with the other girls, but because I was being "elitist" about it. She kicked holes in the walls, punched dents in the refrigerator, lifted the La-Z-Boy recliner up over her head and dropped it onto the living room floor. One night she ripped two feet of drywall out from over the bed. Go sleep with somebody, I said, you'll feel better. She did and I couldn't look at her for a long time. I couldn't even eat. In the end I left her for one of the girls I was sleeping with. To this day she tells every dyke in town and some just passing through that I "physically and emotionally abused" her. Nobody questions her because women don't lie, so my name is mud. Only thing about it, what I learned from Kevin? When somebody you love really *is* hitting you, you don't advertise it, you're too ashamed for letting it happen.

For years I thought, If she won't shut up, could she just move away? She never did. Last spring she had an accident. Trapped in a garage and burnt to a crisp. The other firefighter in there with her? Twenty-some years in the department? He didn't make it. She almost didn't make it either. While she was in the hospital Lydia said, Maybe when she gets out she'll, you know, have seen the light and she'll be nice to you. Are you kidding? I said, When she gets out she'll be a fucking deity, and I was right, she is. Funny thing though, I heard she had to sue the fire department to get in. Discrimination, she claimed, because she couldn't pass the physical.

There were other girls and other lessons. I found out it's important to concentrate on something bad that may or may not have happened to you twenty, thirty years ago, picture it real good in your mind, and relive it on a daily basis. Bring it up when you need an alibi. Say *I don't feel comfortable with that* to make somebody shut up, and *I don't feel safe with that* to make them go away. If somebody catches you with your pants around your ankles say, *You seem to have a problem with trust.*

The same year I read *Woman Hating*, I wrote a story called "Wunna My Fantasies" about a girl in my Incarcerated Women class. I read it to her and she begged me for a copy, so she could act it out with her girlfriend.

I read it to Victoria. She liked it too, because "very few people are willing to admit their rape fantasies, even though everybody has them."

Uh . . . rape? You think this is a story about rape?

She did. I didn't write another story for five years. I became a dogmatic, self-righteous, anti-pornography, anti-S/M, man-hating, black nationalist lesbian separatist. I wrote long-winded, big-worded, angry bitter diatribes about the evil ways of white people that nobody ever saw except my women's studies teachers, who gave me As because it was easier than actually reading my papers. One was published in the black studies journal at San Francisco State. You read it, you don't even know I'm white. I waited for the day I would wake up with brown skin and dreadlocks. It didn't make me happy.

Now I write the way I talk. I write about the people who are in my head and between my legs. I make them do what I want them to do. Sometimes I write friendly stories where everyone cooperates and we all live happily ever after. Other times my stories are mean and vengeful and my ex-girlfriend winds up with shredded bloody tissue where her asshole used to be. That never happened in real life, when I was in love with her.

I wasn't born to grin and bear it, I wasn't born to keep a stiff upper lip, I wasn't born to take it on the chin. I was never meant to hear *Relationships take work, I never wanted to hurt you,* or *Nobody ever said this would be easy,* and I just won't listen to it any more. I was not born to accept hurting as a natural fact.

Now I'm a career-minded, officious, patronizing, intransigent, adversarial prima donna who thinks she deserves special treatment. Ask anybody. Editors make my ass ache. I'm adversarial because I want to get paid.

I'm career-minded, officious, intransigent, patronizing, and a prima donna because I pulled a story after it got picked apart like a boiled chicken, and special treatment means I want my stories to look nice.

I don't like everybody and not everybody likes me. I look for people whose company will soothe me. Most of the time I'm alone. I never say *Don't leave me, I can't live without you,* but sometimes I wish I had somebody who meant that much to me. I hardly ever lie, unless I have to. I want to be known for exactly who I am. I want to have no secrets waiting to be found out. I want to stretch passion to its limits. I want to be rich and famous and hard to find. I want nice things that cost a lot of money. I want to hold my grandchildren in my arms, and I want my daughters to love me again.

AFTER I PUBLISHED my not-rape story in a little magazine for no pay, a judge in Toronto declared it obscene, *The New Yorker* called me a "San Francisco writer who has enjoyed some prominence in the field of lesbian erotica," and Andrea Dworkin, when asked to comment on the judgment, said, "Lesbian porn is an expression of self-hatred."

After the *San Francisco Weekly* published "From Dyke to Dude," my interview with Max Valerio, they received this letter:

> Trish Thomas's article on Max, a female-to-male transsexual featured in a new film by Monika Treut, promulgated some very reactionary ideas about gender. . . . Thomas's article declines to comment on Max's assertion that hormonal treatment has caused him to stop crying, start staring at women in the street, and begin to read magazines like *Penthouse*. The writer never suggests that there could be alternative explanations for the emotional transformations which accompanied Max's use of male hormones such as Max's internalization of social constructions of gender/sex. Consequently, Thomas's article reinforces the decidedly conservative view that complex human behaviors and emotions are determined by biology alone. . . .

Each letter, they told me at the *Weekly*, represents the views of one hundred readers. I also found out through the grapevine that a lot of queer

FTMs (female-to-male transsexuals) think Max is a big stereotypical jerk, and one dyke scenester came up to me and said, Good, you made him sound like the asshole that he is. But a heterosexual playwright told me that my story about Max helped her understand men better.

The truth is, I just let Max sound like Max, and I was fascinated by what he had to say about hormones and living on the other side. I came to the bittersweet awareness that if I were a man, everything about me that brings me grief in the world – the way I walk, the way I talk, the way I think, the way I stand, the way I sit, the way I dress, the way I cut my hair, how much I weigh – would be not only acceptable but revered.

When I first heard that Anita Valerio, the girl Max used to be, was taking hormones to become a man? I felt sorry for her. When more girls in town started doing it, I got pissed off. I called it internalized woman-hating. I said they had low self-esteem, that they'd been brainwashed into hating their female bodies. As I watched them change into men, I began to acknowledge that I wasn't angry so much as envious. I realized if I traded my estrogen for testosterone, I'd get back the two weeks of every month that now go to premenstrual insanity. I'd lose body fat and gain muscle. I wouldn't have to wear dresses to be respectable, I could show up to an interview in a suit and still get the job. People on the bus would stop looking at me like I was a mutant. Even aging would be easier. Older men are craggy and virile and eligible, older women are weak, vulnerable, desperate, and lonely. Becoming a man seemed like the only way for me to make peace with my species. Trouble was, I felt exactly like a woman.

I started lifting weights and stopped sleeping with girls. (I didn't make an announcement, I just stopped, while I was in bed with one.) The combination seems to agree with me. A lot of girls find a home in the dyke community, I never did. Finally giving up on that has allowed me the sense of well-being that comes when you stop trying to gain acceptance into a club that refuses to take you as a member, and looking like I could possibly kick somebody's ass as I now do has stimulated a great deal of respect on the street. Now instead of screaming *Faggot* out their windows when they drive by, young thugs have thoughtful conversations about me.

Damn, I heard from a carful at a stoplight, look at that girl's body.

Pause. Everybody looked. Aw, man, she's just pumped is all.

YOU'RE NOT GONNA BELIEVE THIS, Trish, but women *like* men, Max told me.

No they don't, I thought. What'd they do, take out half your brain when they put in the testosterone? But he's right. Quiet as it's kept in lesbian boot camp, some women do like men, and now I'm one of them. I've gone from wanting to *be* a man to wanting to be *with* a man. I didn't plan it, you can't plan what turns you on, you can only hope it's something you can get.

I told Sallie how my fantasies have gone from fisting a nelly fag drag queen on the kitchen floor of his apartment, to mutual hand jobs with an alternative-type straight boy who secretly craves domination, to being taken hard – stomach to the wall – by a big, beefy, macho dude like Steven Seagal or Sylvester Stallone or Andrew Dice Clay.

But they seem so stupid, she said, what would you talk about?

Nothing, I told her, that's the beauty of it. Even better if I can find one who doesn't speak English.

I did my very first poetry reading at a workshop led by Ntozake Shange. Her musicians played while I read "Don't Ever Sleep with a Lesbian," an epic poem listing all the complaints I had up to the year 1988, at which time *I'd* been sleeping with lesbians for four years. My timing sucked, I was painfully off beat, and the poem definitely "needed work," but I found out what it was like to make a room full of people so quiet you could hear a pin drop. The horn player came up afterward. If that's what it's like, he said, then what difference does it make whether you're with a man or a woman? None, I told him, not when it comes to being treated badly. If he asked me today I'd tell him the difference is a woman can get to places inside you that a man doesn't even know about.

Men *are* different, and I don't care if it's biologically based or the result of gender breeding, I'm ready for a change.

I thought I'd need snappy lines to get along with them, but it's not what you say – they're not listening anyway – it's the feeling you leave them with. It's how they remember the tone of your voice and the way the air felt between you. Women's studies teaches that, intellectually, females are circular and males are linear – they aren't, they don't even think, they sense. Ask a man out and he'll be busy till the year 2000, but sit down close to him, a little bit behind him and off to the side like you don't even know he's there. Let him pick up your scent, feel the heat off your body. Five bucks says when you walk out the door he'll be waiting on the sidewalk, hoping you come out alone.

I've found that I can stare at a man in the gym, looking as sultry as I know how, willing him to know I want him, and he'll look at me like I just killed his mother, because he doesn't think for a minute that a girl like me could be interested in a guy like him. But if I walk over and ask him to spot me – I usually have to say it twice before he can believe I'm actually talking to him – his face softens, and his shoulders drop. All of a sudden he's ready to take care of me. Angel calls this letting him know he's more of a man than I am. If him being more of a man than me means we can get cozy without getting clammy, I am there.

A mother I know told me she had no maternal feelings whatsoever until after she had an abortion, then she wanted to have a baby more than anything else in the world. I didn't like men until I hated them. I didn't hate women until I loved them.

One thing worries me. Statistics show that the average heterosexual sexual act consists of nine strokes per minute for a total of four minutes, or a grand total of thirty-six strokes. If this is true, I was robbed. I don't remember ever once getting a complete thirty-six strokes. (Maybe I *was* a lesbian because I just never found the right man.) A woman can lie and cheat and steal the sheets out from under you as good as any dude, but at least she'll keep going until you're done. Angel says, The thing to remember is, if it's bad, you don't have to do it again. Lydia says, Don't just lie there like some girls.

Maybe this time next year I'll be thinking about being a dude again, or maybe I'll do a full 180 back to lesbian separatism. Maybe sex with men will still suck so bad I'll have to move on to horses or dolphins or chimpanzees. All I know for sure is, I won't be the same person then that I am now. Things change. If they didn't, I'd still be wearing high heels and Sheer Energy panty hose.

CLOSE ENCOUNTERS
(BUT NO CIGAR) ----------------------------

QUEEN FOR A DAY ——

Persimmon Blackbridge

&

Susan Stewart

are two of three members of the Kiss & Tell Col-

lective of writers and video and visual artists

based in Vancouver. Their performance pieces

have been staged in cities across Canada and in

the United States, and their work has been exhib-

ited in North America and in Europe. Individually

and together, they have contributed to numerous

books and anthologies.

It was 1968 and I hated high school. I hated it so bad they sent me to the school shrink, who didn't help. He sat behind his desk with his gray suit and pursed lips and wrote mysterious notes. Freudian analysis maybe, or shopping lists. He didn't like me. He didn't like my grades or my attitude or my psychedelic miniskirts. I'm not sure what my diagnosis was – probably Bad Kid.

Besides my school shrink, I had a downtown social worker, who was a different proposition altogether. He was an anarchist Yippie (not to be confused with yuppie) who had somehow managed to get conscientious-objector status from his draft board and was doing alternative service as a youth worker for the City of Chicago. He picked me up one afternoon wandering stoned down Clark Street, and although I wasn't a runaway like most of his "clients," he figured I could do better for myself. He was right about that, because my life at the time consisted of hating high school, taking too many drugs, and having joyless sex with any

Two weeks after my mother died, my father's sister took me shopping for a new dress. I cannot remember this dress, although I do recall the shop, women's clothes on the second floor, the conservative feeling of the place, the racks of unappealing attire, the hideous reality of his venture and my quiet desperation. There is a photo of my high school graduation and perhaps I am wearing the dress for this occasion. It is white with a lavender floral print, small purple buttons gathering at the bust, princess style. I have shortened the full skirt into a mini, the sole application of my home economics skills. I courted the inevitable disapproval of my elders but I was reckless. I knew they wouldn't chastise the bereaved.

With summer came the lofty position of arts and crafts leader at a camp for rich girls. I was terrified of the girls, who were only slightly younger than me, and spent all my free time hiding out in the crafts house, surrounded by the smell of crayons and glue, seeking oblivion through sleep. Evenings were boy who asked (while dreaming of girls).

Anyway, Dennis (that was his name) decided that I needed something more in my life: more challenging than high school and more fun than bad sex. Political activism. I don't know how he wrote it up in his reports to his supervisor, but in real life, he took me to Yippie organizing meetings and guerrilla theater actions and the Students for a Democratic Society Radical Education Centre (aka the SDS REC House), where most of the Chicago SDS staff both lived and worked. I started feeling better immediately. He was an excellent social worker.

My parents (old lefties themselves) approved of Dennis. He was clearly better

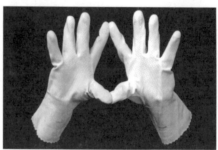

than the school shrink. But they didn't approve of my habit of staying out until the buses stopped running and then calling home and asking if I could stay the night. Dennis was a single man and I was not allowed to spend the night at his place, even though he never fucked his "clients" and was too paranoid to allow drugs in his house (a tough act for a Yippie to pull off and still maintain his reputation as a cool dude, but he did). I was, however, allowed to spend the night at the REC House, where drugs ran riot and most of the boys collected girls on principle ("fucking her into the Movement," it was called). But girls also lived there: Sage and Red and Kathy, and my best friend Marilyn, an older

spent with boys who had cars and, if I was lucky, drugs. We were rural townies and we were fast.

In the fall I went to college. Classes were incidental to the main event, which was the advanced and enthusiastic pursuit of "cool" and escape through drugs and sex. In no way could I entertain the idea of being straight (i.e., not stoned). It was too close to being "real," and this calamity was to be avoided at all costs. I had chosen this college because the name of the town in which it was situated matched that of a village in a book of fantasy, one that in earlier years had provided me with hours of escape. Escape was a major theme of my youth, and I was very tuned in to symbolic correspondences.

The college culture that I gravitated toward consisted of a handful of somewhat eccentric personalities. Most of us were from rural communities, with the exception of a few sophisticated urbanites, and all of us were new to the world of Intellect and Culture. It was the early seventies and the air was thick with ideas like Marxism, socialism, civil rights, revolution, and women's liberation. Until this point my major source of information on these matters had been TV and parental reaction, which, in regards to women's lib, had been swift and pointed.

woman (twenty-six) whom my parents relied on to take care of me. Of course I never explained the facts of life in SDS to them or told them about how many hippies got beat up in the disputed territories I passed through on my Saturday-night walks from Dennis's to the REC House. Why would I?

Now comes the feminism part.

One Sunday morning I was wandering around the REC House, reading political pamphlets

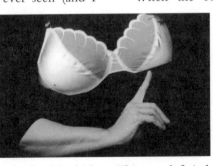

and generally amusing myself. Everyone else was still wrapped in their sleeping bags, dreaming of revolution, or recovering from the night before. In the kitchen, I discovered the most amazing huge and impressive mountain of unwashed dishes I had ever seen (and I had been around). There were pans of baked-on brown rice and plates of petrified soybean casserole and cups of molding herbal tea. Cool! I often won myself points with the big kids by doing various household chores, but this was above and beyond. I would be Miss Popularity for days! I found a not-too-disgusting pair of rubber gloves (for prevention of disease only) and dug in.

An hour later, I was still deep in dishwater but the pile was much diminished.

Everybody knew about bra-burners, and we all agreed they were a stupid embarrassment. My one experiment with going without had been utterly mortifying and I was not eager for a repeat performance. Nevertheless, among my new circle of friends were a couple of women with some very rad ideas. Sally was an insomniac, and in opposition to the state she would periodically overturn the dorm concession machine in the middle of the night and empty it of change. Another girl, Jane, was becoming seriously enthusiastic about women's lib. This made her un-cool, but from a loyalty born out of our shared highs, I was loath to drop her.

When the college announced its annual homecoming queen beauty pageant and Jane said "we" should protest, I knew I was in trouble. When Sally agreed I realized I was in *big* trouble. This was definitely not going to be cool, but I reluctantly agreed to go along since there didn't seem to be any room for choice in the matter. I wasn't anti-beauty, though. I had stopped shaving my legs but deep down I thought hairy legs were gross. Was I secretly jealous I didn't get asked to run for beauty queen?

In the rest of the house, morning noises were starting up. A door opened, then closed. The toilet flushed. Red came stumbling into the kitchen in an ancient pink terry-cloth robe, searching for coffee. She looked up and saw me, the dishes, my big, smug smile.

Her expression of stupefied sleepiness transformed into righteous rage in one electrified second.

I didn't understand why she was yelling at me. I didn't understand why she pulled Kathy and Sage out of bed and into the kitchen where they started yelling at me too. Marilyn followed close behind, shut the door in the boys' faces, and tried to explain.

"It's like a protest. We're sick of the guys never cleaning up, so we're refusing to wash the dishes until they start doing their share."

"But I don't mind washing the dishes," I said. "I like to!"

(My mother would have been amazed at this information.)

"Well that's fine, but right now we're on strike," Marilyn explained.

"Which makes you a scab for the Patriarchy," Kathy added. Kathy was the top chick in Chicago SDS, the one

Nope, not that, although there was some stigma or social myth currently running that said only the ugly girls were women's libbers. Word was that bitterness drove them to it when they couldn't get a man. Was I already bitter at nineteen because I didn't have a boyfriend?

Jane had studied women's lib protests by watching them on the TV news. She knew what we had to do. We were to dress up as beauty queens ourselves, as extreme queens, queens from hell. This was to include giant breasts, enormous hips, ridiculous clothes, wigs, makeup, and placards. "What will our signs say?" I innocently inquired, dreading the inevitable answer. "Down with the Patriarchy," fist in the woman's symbol, "Women's Rights Now," and other phrases garnered from TV and *Time* magazine. This was getting worse by the minute. My only consolation was the slim hope that my queen-y disguise would work. Maybe, just maybe, nobody would recognize me.

What my conspiratorial friends didn't know was that another friend, a very hip chick from Montreal and a classmate in art, was a serious contender for who always made big public speeches and got into arguments at conferences. Not the kind of person you'd want to be called a scab for the Patriarchy by. She was pacing the kitchen floor. She should have been wearing tall boots with loud heels, but even in bedroom slippers she made the room seem somehow smaller. Kathy often had strange effects on interior design.

I was backed against the sink, feeling deeply confused, my hands suddenly sweating in the rubber gloves. "You're tired of doing the dishes by yourselves, but you don't want me to do them for you? I don't get it."

"We want the guys to do their share," Marilyn explained.

"We want a little goddamn equality in this goddamn house," Kathy added.

I tried to come up with an articulate and politically astute argument. I tried to look cool and thoughtful, but the rubber gloves got in the way. "OK, but like what does it matter who does the dishes, if it's a guy or a girl? Whoever has the energy for them should do them. Like if one person is uptight about dirty dishes and another person isn't – "

"Jesus Christ on a crutch! Don't be such a suck-ass liberal." Throwing me a look of aggravation bordering on femicide, Kathy swept out the door, followed by Red and Sage.

the title of homecoming queen. She would never speak to me again if she knew I was protesting against the pageant and neither would any of her sophisticated circle of friends, whose acceptance I secretly coveted. I was doomed. Damned if I did and damned if I didn't, but ultimately susceptible to peer pressure. I was going to do it.

To this day I can't remember much about the event itself. Being inexperienced protesters, we neglected to inform the media about our impending "action," so there wasn't any documentation. I remember tottering to the auditorium in borrowed stilettoes with five other "queens." I remember occupying a kind of circular dais in the lobby which was full of leafy plants, we six its exotic flowers. The general public filing by in full formal dress, looking at us askance with both pity and disgust registering in their well-educated and liberal eyes. Profs, their wives, students, and parents, all pretending we didn't exist, the blight on an otherwise unblemished tradition.

I recall my out-of-body experience brought on by a confusing mix of the deepest mortification and shame, and an unfamiliar feeling that was akin to a carnival ride. I experienced a thrill that tickled some undeveloped region of my being, something I could describe now

"It's Women's Liberation," Marilyn explained patiently. She had a husband and two kids somewhere back in Minnesota and was good at patience.

"Huh?" I said.

"Did you ever wonder why it's always the chicks who end up doing the housework? Or why the guys always write the leaflets and we always type them?"

"Kathy writes leaflets," I pointed out. "It's not whether you're a chick, it's whether you have a leaflet-writing personality."

"But why is Kathy the only one?"

"She has an unusual personality. For a girl."

Marilyn kept trying. She was my friend.

But it took four more years until I was down and desperate enough, flat-out crazy enough, to suffer the confusing, infuriating, exhilarating, miserable wrench of consciousness, to start looking at the world from the point of view of women.

I felt better immediately.

as being my first taste of the power of resistance. Despite the public humiliation, the fear of visible opposition, the pain of social rejection – despite all that, something felt good. I could tell, when I dared lift my eyes off the floor, that the other girls felt it too. We started to twinkle at the edges. We were brave and we knew we were brave. There was something to protest here, and if it wasn't beauty, well then, it was blandness. We were pathetic to these people, laughingstocks, our "cause" ridiculous, but we twinkled and sparkled to one another.

Aline Kominsky-Crumb

Female underground comics pioneer Aline Kominsky-Crumb's revolutionary

autobiographical strips have been collected in *Love That Bunch*, published

in 1990. *Dirty Laundry*, released in 1993, brings together the

comics she and her husband, cartoonist Robert Crumb,

created together over an eighteen-year period.

She and her husband and daughter

Sophie (also a cartoonist) live

in the south of France.

faites votre choix...

SALLIE TISDALE

is an award-winning essayist and author of five nonfiction books, including, most recently, *Talk Dirty to Me.* Her work has appeared in *Harper's, The New Republic, The New Yorker*, and other magazines. She lives in the US Northwest.

CLICK

My parents slept in a small room in the back of the house, where gray vinyl blinds were perpetually drawn against the day. A double bed and two cluttered dressers nearly filled the floor. Sometimes I sat on the bed while Mom put away clothes, shoving them into a closet stuffed like a turkey with my father's slacks and shirts. We talked of this and that and I fiddled with her costume jewelry and looked at her collection of dolls, and sometimes I helped. My mother was one of the few women I knew who had a job; she taught fifth grade at my elementary school. In the afternoon we watched *The Mike Douglas Show* and *Lost in Space* together, and in the evenings she corrected papers and called parents and made study plans. Her weekend hours were for housework, and most of our time together was spent on grocery shopping, ironing, vacuuming, and laundry.

One day, a sunny day in spring when I was nine, I came running in the way I often did to tell her I was going off somewhere with my big brother, with whom I went everywhere – up to the hillside to catch lizards or chase rabbits, down the muddy culverts where the creek ran, over to the park to climb the pitch-sticky cedar trees. She never minded, always a little distracted, her mind on many things. But this time, she said no.

Childhood is like a silent film, the subtitles removed – a jerky, dramatic story unfolding again and again before our eyes, the words lost, meanings misconstrued. Even names become confused. After a time, memory and imagination weave together so tightly it's impossible to tell which is which. Why is that person laughing? Who is speaking? Whose hand is that, holding mine? Why am I standing beside a Christmas tree in my pajamas, holding a ragged toy? So we remember. And I remember my mother with great clarity; she is intensely familiar and near; I can mimic each turn and gesture, each tilt of her head. But I'll never know if I remember her or only who she seemed, to me, to be.

She resisted marriage and children until she finished college, and was older than the mothers of my friends, whose houses were neater and more nicely decorated than our own. In our house, laundry and dishes perpetually spilled out of their proper places. She was a plain woman who disguised her nerves behind books and her longings in her work, who finally knew she'd best not wait any longer and married my brooding, handsome father as soon as they graduated from college. She stands straight and proud in the class picture from her first teaching job in a poor rural mountain school. She was already pregnant, and eventually she had to quit that job because she had three children in her first five years of marriage. And then – plain, weary, overworked – she went back to teaching. I remember her behind her desk, and in the smoky teacher's lounge, and on the playground of our elementary school. But often when I think of her, I remember her folding clothes – her clothes, my father's clothes, my clothes, my brother's clothes, my sister's clothes, towels, sheets, pillowcases, even doll clothes – and all around her in the cramped bedroom, my father's flung-off dirty things waiting to be washed again. She didn't complain, only folded – efficiently flipping sleeves in, rolling socks together, creasing pants into pleats. She showed me how to fold sheets alone, holding the long lengths of worn cotton in drapes over my arm, using every finger and my chin. But I preferred to do it with her, by halves and quarters, so that the sheet collapsed in a few seconds to a neat square to put on the pile we'd made.

On this spring day, she said, No, it's time you started acting like a girl. Time to stop playing with the boys. I talked back – I always talked back, no matter what. I said I wished I *was* a boy. And she stopped folding and looked at me and said, Someday you'll be glad you're a girl. You can do something your brother can never do. Someday you can have a baby.

I DIDN'T STOP CHASING MY BROTHER for years, not until he left in misery for a military academy to make my father proud. But I gave up the cedar trees and culverts. I traded them for motorcycles and jacked-up cars driven by men years older than me whose last names I never knew. I traded them for books and songs – about revolution, authority, change. I was a sea of opposing tides, bewildering compulsions, appetites, and loneliness. I became a girl without any quality of girlishness, the kind of girl that makes her father mad and keeps her mother up nights.

I filled up with love affairs – affairs with politics, God, romance, protests, with my own opinions, with possibility, with boys, with girls. I fought with every teacher, with every command, with every expectation. I refused familiar guidance, looking always away, beyond, to ideas and people distant from home. I went alone to the family doctor when I was just sixteen, got the pill, and started sleeping with my boyfriend. A few months later, over my father's angry demands, I left home for good.

I went to college. I joined committees and collectives. I wrote bad poetry, and a few good paragraphs, and made elaborate plans for new and better communities, schools, and ways of life. I fell in love: with Tom, Carol, Lisa, Terry. I moved farther away and I never called my mother.

I read Betty Friedan and Betty Dodson and *Ms.* magazine and *Our Bodies, Ourselves,* and stopped taking the pill. At seventeen, the pill seemed like an old woman's choice. I went alone to the college infirmary to have a Copper-7 IUD inserted. In less than a week the copper hook embedded in my uterine walls like a gaff, and, infected and feverish, I went to the hospital. I was not quite eighteen, and when I came out of surgery I found myself on the pediatrics ward, my mother beside me. My father silently stalked the halls. When I told her the doctor had said I might never be able to get pregnant now, she just looked at me and didn't say anything at all.

I began to volunteer at a women's health center. I learned to use a speculum, read a cervix, interpret the slowly falling sand of a pregnancy test. I fell in love with Nancy. I fell in love with Clyde. I fell in love with Bill, and then Connie, and then Connie's boyfriend, and he fell in love with me. I had another surgery, and another, always in pain, never quite well, as though the copper fishhook was still in me, the wound still festering, not quite clean. I got slowly worse. When I was nineteen, a doctor told me to get pregnant if I could. Now or never, he said. And then another doctor said the same thing. Now or never. I asked a friend with three children how she'd known she was ready to be a mother and she said, Honey, you're never ready.

I stopped going to meetings. I started working for a living. Connie's boyfriend got me pregnant, and Nancy did the test at the women's health center, and we stood in a circle and cheered. A year later I was living with my infant son in a one-room apartment. I was working for a children's protective agency, shepherding abused children from their foster homes to see their angry parents for an hour or so under my watchful eye. I was fond of wearing a т-shirt that said, "Every mother is a working mother." When my baby was nine months old, I got a hysterectomy, and then I got college grants and student loans and even a scholarship or two, and food stamps, and sometimes my mother sent me a check. I went to classes, and late at night I tried to write stories.

I began going to political meetings again, women's meetings, hauling my baby along. I started volunteering at another women's clinic, and joined a health collective, and wrote for an alternative newspaper, and fell half in love with my best friend, Karen, who read me Olga Broumas poems out loud. One day, a sunny day in spring, I sat in a group of lesbian separatists and listened to them discuss whether to offer free child care to male children as well as female ones. They decided to care only for the girls, and I felt my heart tear like my uterus, and I left and didn't go back.

I fell in love again, with a man, and when we were married and ready for our first dance at the reception, I asked the band to play "You Can't Always Get What You Want." I finished college ten years after I'd started. We adopted an older boy and a little girl, and at thirty, I was as weary as my mother had ever been, working and raising three children in a two-bedroom house, folding mountains of laundry, wondering what, if anything, came next.

I thought I would be embarrassed to tell these stories, because for many years I was embarrassed that children mattered to me, that I slipped with such surprising ease into a niche shaped much like my mother's. Embarrassed to bring my husband to meet Karen and her lover Carlotta, twins in their black leather jackets and smug smiles, laughing at our bickering domesticity. Embarrassed by my own ordinary appearance, by what doesn't show, by what no longer holds true. Embarrassed at how it set me apart.

But I'm not, not at all. From well before I got pregnant I was ambivalent, but that's another thing – it's like being sometimes certain, and it never goes entirely away. The rearing of children and the enormous work they require goes on and on, for months and then years and then decades. Sometimes I think the work will never end, even as they pummel at me to get away, to stand up, take off. But again and again I'm glad for it, for how it opened me up cleanly, like a scalpel cutting out the dirty wound, for how it broke me like a horse is broken, who learns to love its master. Take off, I tell them now, but for all the cutting of ties between mother and child they are bound to me and I am bound to them.

My mother died when my daughter could barely stand. I've taught her since how to fold sheets with me, a duet of halves and quarters, collapsing to a square, one more for the pile we've made.

COMING

Unclicked

—

Naomi

KLEIN

Naomi Klein

is a writer and editor. She writes a weekly nationally syndicated column in the *Toronto Star* and is the former editor of *This Magazine*, Canada's leading alternative periodical. Her writing has appeared in the *Globe and Mail*, *Ms.* magazine, the *Village Voice*, *Elm Street*, and *The Baffler*, and her forthcoming book, *No Logo*, will be published in 1998 by Knopf. She lives in Toronto.

CLAUDETTE had a tiny black-and-white television in her dorm room. We sat in a semicircle, inches away from it; four of us cross-legged on the floor and on the edge of her futon.

The newscast was chaotic: a mad gunman had gone on a shooting rampage at the University of Montreal, a campus six hours away in the hometown I had left four months before. The death count wasn't confirmed but he had killed over a dozen students, then turned the gun on himself. Sirens, bodies loaded into ambulances, crowds of people, snow, slush, more sirens. There was one image that flashed on the screen over and over again: a young woman sitting at a table, her body limp, her head hanging back, neck exposed. Shot dead in the university cafeteria.

Slowly the reports started taking shape. Thirteen students and one university employee were confirmed dead. All were women. There was no explanation given for this at first but the reporter did mention that as the gunman separated the men from the women in the classroom, he told his prey, "You're all a bunch of fucking feminists." Then he killed them.

Feminists, the reports later told us, because they were women who had decided to study engineering, a traditionally male-dominated field. Feminists, because the gunman, Marc Lépine, had wanted to be an engineer, but he hadn't been admitted to the program. To his deranged mind, his spot had gone to one of these fucking feminists.

We looked at one another, at our crossed legs, at the floor beneath us. We imagined the frozen, deserted courtyards where we would walk the next day, the classrooms and lecture halls and dining rooms of the University of Toronto where we, and thousands of other young women, were doing this thing that most of us never questioned: getting an education, studying to be doctors, lawyers, journalists, scientists, and engineers.

The meaning of going to university changed dramatically on the night of December 6, 1989. Our very presence in this closet-sized dorm room felt suddenly subversive. We were acutely aware of how obvious we were being about it – hanging out in groups of other women students, living in residence, going to class, to the library, even. Not very subtle camouflage if someone wants to blow your brains out for being female and at university.

We felt like sitting ducks, targets waiting for the gunshots. Why? Because we were women. No other reason. Nothing else to talk about. Terror after all doesn't discriminate; it isn't interested in your political motivations, in your angst, in how different and individual you really are. One thing mattered to Marc Lépine about his victims and one thing only: they were women.

That night went on forever, spilling into other rooms and dark hallways. We told stories – horrifying ones about incest, rape, and violent boyfriends. It seemed like every woman I talked to that night was a victim of male violence. I told my friends that when I was thirteen, I had been raped, only I didn't call it that at the time. "He forced himself on me" was the phrase of choice back then. It was at a party, I was plastered. My whole high school knew about the incident but I had never told the story quite like this before. Now my story wasn't just about a bad night or an asshole guy, or my sordid past – it was evidence of a conspiracy. Telling it made me feel strangely powerful. Valid. Real.

More high school images flashed in my head – boyfriends who "loved" me so much it made them want to shake and push me; my bizarre pride in death-defyingly low math grades; years spent on the phone performing in-depth Freudian analyses on my classmates. How much time, exactly, I wondered, had I wasted sticking my fingers down my throat until the knuckles were raw? How many hours had I waited twenty-two minutes until the peroxide had bleached my hair? All the while, the boys I knew were out playing hockey or learning to debate or having hobbies or having lives.

In my last years of high school, I finally decided to use my brain. My mind raced to the pot-smoking, philosophy-reading boys who sneeringly wrote off all the girls at my predominantly Jewish school as JAPs – unevolved bimbos who couldn't do anything but gossip, apply copious amounts of makeup, and maybe, at best, give head. I spent months convincing them that I was different. I trashed my former female friends relentlessly and savagely until finally, I was allowed to be the smart girl. On the night of the Montreal massacre, it struck me that I had spent years selling out my gender, that my desire to be the exception was just more self-hatred. And I hated those boys for making me do it.

In a moment I rewrote my life with Marc Lépine's eyes: everything that happened to me wasn't about the complicated mesh of reasons that I had always believed – fate, stupidity, laziness, cowardice, and even (sometimes) my own intelligence – it was all about gender. I was a woman, not an individual. Everything that had ever happened to me was determined by this biological fact. How could I have been so blind?

My friend Kyo says when I became a feminist that night, it had the force of a dam breaking. She said it to me that very night in the hall, overwhelmed by the tide of epiphanies streaming from my mouth. It does sound cartoonish, this moment of clarity. And in many ways, it was. To all the people around me – and for many years, to myself – the night of the Montreal massacre was my very own moment of radicalization. My "click."

But the truth is that feminism wasn't something that came to me that night. It was something I have lived with my whole life, woven deeply into my childhood, into my family home, like Judaism. My mother is a feminist and she raised me to be one, but before the massacre, I had resisted it with the fervor of a political prisoner (which, in a way, I was). On the night Marc Lépine shot those fourteen women, I raced back into my mother's arms for the first time in my nineteen-year-long life. Some radical.

"ALL THE TITS AND ASSES were all lined up for her to see. What could she think of her own self and her own little body surrounded by this?" That rhetorical question is at the beginning of *Not a Love Story*, an internationally acclaimed feminist film about pornography released in 1980. My mother, Bonnie Sherr Klein, directed and narrated the film. The little body in question was mine.

My mother explained – first in the film, then on every talk show from *Alan Thicke* to *Good Morning America* – that she had decided to make *Not a Love Story* after taking her eight-year-old daughter Naomi to the corner store to buy bus tickets. There she noticed me looking at the racks of porn magazines and wondered how they made me feel.

I'm pretty sure I never thought much about how pictures of naked women made me feel. Probably a little weird, maybe a little bit curious. I did find out, however, how it felt to have a mother make films with dirty pictures, and what it was like to try to disappear into the cans of ravioli as she got into yet another argument with a convenience store clerk about the placement of *Hustler* magazine. To a deeply conformist kid (who spent most of her fantasy life dreaming of circle driveways and Kool-Aid moms) it was the height of humiliation.

I hated *Not a Love Story* with every fiber of my being even before the film was finished. It started when my mother – who felt guilty about being away so much – brought me to work with her at the National Film Board, where she was screening the rushes. I spent my days off from Grade Four watching hours of strip acts, clips from hard-core porn films, and live sex shows on 42nd Street.

I also watched interviews with feminists who said that these images were acts of violence against all women, that the only response to these *other* women – the strippers and porn actresses – was outrage and resistance. "To be female and conscious anywhere on the planet is to be in a constant state of rage," Robin Morgan told the camera, tears streaming down her face. Over and over again, the feminists said there was a war going on. A war against women. The enemy's tools were naked pictures.

Of course *Not a Love Story* attempted to distinguish between pornography and erotica, but those subtleties were way over my head. I remember watching the footage of Kate Millett's charcoal sketches of breasts and asses. My mother bought one – it hung in our bathroom for years: a single curved line with a dot/nipple floating at the top. "Sometimes it feels like you're on top of the world" is scrawled across it. That was a "good" sexual image. That and the Georgia O'Keeffe flower/vagina over my parents' bed.

I didn't understand why a line with a dot on it was sexy but naked women dancing and grinding was violence. I thought these women were beautiful and I liked to watch them, particularly Lindalee Tracy, the Montreal stripper who "starred" in the film. Even though my mother and Lindalee became good friends, I knew I wasn't really supposed to admire her. There was something wrong with Lindalee – she was part of the pornography. But she was also the only one of my mother's friends who treated me like I was real; she asked me questions about boys and school as if she really cared and knew exactly what I meant. Plus, she was young and pretty and wore tight jeans.

Not like the "good" feminists in *Not a Love Story*. I thought they were an abomination. I couldn't stand to look at their terrible clothes or their wild gray hair. I'm embarrassed now by my conventional ideas about beauty and femininity, that I didn't see the halo that surrounds Susan Griffin or the grace of Margaret Atwood, but I didn't. I just saw my mother, whose hippie clothes and touchy-feely style made me dread the idea of bringing friends home. To my nine-year-old eyes, feminists were the gatekeepers protecting me from the world of strippers, pornos, peep shows, and naked people – the world of sex.

Sex and violence became so intertwined in these screenings that I started fearing men in my own family and our closest friends. Gradually, I developed such a severe phobia of male intruders that I secretly turned my room into a fortress with an arsenal of makeshift weapons – vases, brushes, and knives – all hidden around my bed.

When the film was finally finished and we held a private family screening, I walked out halfway through. I resolved never to watch *Not a Love Story* in its entirety and to boycott all of the publicity. I announced that I would never go to another rally or march, or allow myself to be dragged to another meeting. I didn't quite understand what these events were about but I knew that when I went to them, I was an accessory to my mother's politics and that my choice, and my individuality, were stripped away.

I also did the worst thing possible to get my revenge: I became a no-holds-barred Girl. There were no jeans tight enough, no peroxide powerful enough, no eyeliner electric enough. There were more hazardous forms of teenage rebellion than hyper-femininity – and I experimented with most of those as well – but not in my house.

AMONG MY GROUP OF FRIENDS, calling yourself a feminist after the Montreal massacre was considered an act of defiance against Marc Lépine and everything he represented. We would give ourselves the label that he had spat at his victims before he massacred them. And we would wear it not as an epithet but as a badge of honor.

Not everyone agreed with this sentiment, however. Some women complained that they didn't like labels; they would say "I'm not a feminist but . . ." or "I'm a humanist." We ridiculed them as traitors. After years of compulsive self-analysis, I was seeing complexity, intellectual honesty, and self-knowledge as a sign of weakness. Any woman whose primary identification wasn't with her gender was a weak bitch.

About a month after the massacre, I watched *Not a Love Story* again. This time, it all made sense. I saw the stock-in-trade porn images – the back arched, the head thrown back, the throat exposed – for what they really were: the girl in the cafeteria at the University of Montreal, shot dead for being a woman who wanted something better.

The truth is that after the massacre I saw violence everywhere. It destroyed my emotional shock absorbers. My body tensed when a male student reached into his bag in class – I thought he would pull out a gun. I scanned subway platforms, trying to pick out the psycho who would push me onto the tracks. Just as Lépine wanted to kill the generic woman, I became terrified of the generic man. Each and every one of them. Just like when I was nine.

It was hard not to blame all men for the Montreal massacre – in part because so many men seemed to blame themselves. In print and in person, there was an outpouring of guilt. "I have Marc Lépine in me" was their chest-beating rallying cry, and if they didn't say it, we said they were pigs. How dare these men try to take responsibility solely for their own actions? How dare they insist they had always treated women fairly, never committed an act of violence? It seemed for a while that we would not be satisfied until every man admitted he was a would-be rapist or murderer. In retrospect, that prospect fills me with hopelessness, but at the time, there was much joy in momentary surges of power.

It was the first time, conversely, that I had ever seen men give up power. Suddenly they were handing it over to us in buckets – with a ribbon around it (a white ribbon, that is, as many men now wear to mark the anniversary of the Montreal massacre). So why stop at a mere admission of guilt? We flexed our new could-be-victims muscles all over the place; we banned men from vigils, from women's centers and from newly formed women's caucuses. "This is a war zone," we said.

I, who had screamed and sulked and threatened when my parents sent me to an all-girls school in Grade Nine, now kicked out the men every chance I got. Better yet, after years of merciless, and often abusive, self-improvement projects, I could finally hold the mirror up to someone else's face and say: "It's you. You are the problem."

I think the frantic mood on campus after the massacre would have subsided if there hadn't been so much ammunition to fuel our rage. The more conservative students were infuriated by feminism's new powers of persuasion, and after I edited a special issue of the student newspaper on the anniversary of that horrific night, a group of engineers broke into our offices, vandalized the building, and left a rape threat for me. Several other outspoken campus feminists were sent anonymous death threats. "Marc Lépine was right," the notes declared. To me and my friends, it seemed like everyone wanted us to shut up – proof positive that we should keep screaming.

We also did our part to keep the temperature high. Studies that claimed one in four university-age women had been sexually assaulted – a term that included everything from a pat on the ass to forced intercourse at knifepoint – were magically transformed on posters to "one in four women have been raped." I threw myself into the prevention of all of these would-be assaults. We turned campus Orientation Week into a festival of date-rape awareness – it was our very own feminist hazing ritual. We filled the first issue of the student newspaper with how-to manuals on not getting raped: don't get drunk at parties, don't go to a guy's room, make sure somebody knows where you are. As I churned out these warnings, the person I always imagined reading them was me – my former high school self. She was so weak and unwise, that girl, not at all like the woman I was now. And that's how I became safe – by scaring the shit out of everybody else.

Although I still believe we had the best of intentions, all of our feminist crusades from that time were infused with an alarming casualness about such legal technicalities as freedom of speech and the rights of the accused. Like so many feminist exterminators, we tried to rid the campus of all sexist matter: newspapers published by the engineering society, pin-up girls, letters to the editor, and even the use of certain words. Some women wrote lists of alleged rapists on the bathroom walls. We had never met these men, but we were ready to destroy them on the hearsay of women we had never met either.

Of all these excesses, the one I find most disturbing is an essay I wrote outlining my new theories on heterosexual love (it was a women's studies course – you could do that sort of thing). I argued that to make up for society's sexism, the man should relinquish all of his power to the woman. The only way this unfortunate hypothetical pair could have nonviolent sex was if the guy was never on top. The missionary position, after all, was the physical embodiment of patriarchy.

Where did this theory come from? Not from my heart, not from my sex life. I have never wanted that kind of power and it slips through my fingers to the floor whenever anyone tries to hand it to me. Reading the essay now, I feel like I do watching *Not a Love Story*: disembodied. Desire so rarely obeys rhetoric – no matter how well reasoned. Theorizing about the politics and morality of sex is dangerous territory. Like mother, like daughter, I guess.

LATELY, I feel myself becoming unclicked – unhinged, like a crazy person. As economic disparities become more acute, I'm finding it harder and harder to accept that gender wars are at all constructive. I argue incessantly with the person I was after the massacre and, unlike taking on the sexist bastards, there is no joy in being right. There are no groups or centers for me to join. No rooms filled with women waiting to share stories and hand me a ready-made life complete with a fully stocked library, political posters, and goddess earrings. None that I would want to join, anyway.

On the sixth anniversary of the Montreal massacre, I watched the vigils on television. A nineteen-year-old university student was being interviewed, her face mummied in scarf and hat and her gloved hand shielding a candle from the freezing wind. I know that girl, I thought, though I had never seen her before. She was telling the reporter that the massacre was not the act of a lone madman, but was on the extreme end of a continuum of violence against women for which all men are responsible and under which all women are victims. I found myself cursing at the TV screen: there *is* such a thing as an individual, we are *not* all symbolic representatives of our gender in *your* women's studies course. Violent men exist – I have known them, I have been locked underneath them – but they are *not all men*.

At first I wanted to be wrong, I tried to find people to convince me again: How do we know women don't lie? – I once knew one who did. Tell me again why affirmative action isn't discrimination. What about all the powerful women – where do they fit into patriarchy? What about all the poor, weak, and victimized men? Are you sure it's all about gender? What about globalization? How about plain old capitalist exploitation?

As I furtively read the new wave of Paglia-inspired feminist-bashers, I seize on the gaping flaws in their arguments, and on their alarming lack of compassion. But part of me is also attracted to these women who brag that they (unlike those weak and prudish feminists) *aren't* afraid of the dark, can handle any sexist pig who pats their ass, don't need any special privileges to get jobs, and even enjoy a little porn in their spare time. Feminism is about finding your strength, and I know I'm that strong too.

Still, I'm not ready to sign up for the embittered backlash. It reminds me too much of my sixteen-year-old self, getting in with the guys by viciously trashing my female friends. I guess I'm not so arrogant as to have forgotten that I wasn't always this strong.

One thing has crossed over in me for certain, though: I don't want to be defined by my gender – not by men and not by other women. For me, feminism has become a tool I bring with me, not a place to stay put.

sonja

mills

Sonja Mills

m.ills

is a Toronto writer, playwright, and actor and the author of four stage plays, including the much-acclaimed *Dyke City Trilogy* and *101 Things Lesbians Do in Bed*, which has enjoyed sold-out runs in Toronto and Vancouver. Her poetry, prose, and porn have been published in numerous magazines and anthologies.

MY FIRST FEMINIST OUTRAGE occurred as a result of inadvertently discovering, at the age of eleven, that my brother's underpants were so much more comfortable than my own. So commodious, so unrestricting! No painful lesions on the innerest of inner thighs from too-tight elastic, no wedgies when I walked. My resolve was great. From this day forward, I would wear no undergarment deemed "dainty" by its manufacturer; I would don no panty, pantalette, ladies' brief, nor bloomer. Indeed, I would clothe

screaming

myself in no unmentionable that was not clearly intended for use by the opposite sex. But by the time I entered university in the early eighties, having eagerly learned everything I knew about women's liberation from watching *Maude* on TV, I was primed for a much greater emancipation than that which my choice of gotchies could ever afford.

The women at my college were stalwart and intense, and had much loftier concerns than the girls I knew in high school, whose priorities were looking pretty and finding boyfriends. Unfortunately, since none of my new colleagues wore brassieres or did housework, being well versed in Beatrice Arthur's antediluvian brand of feminism was of little use to me. I knew nothing of the issues these women so eloquently and passionately discussed, but I was determined to pursue this thing called "a feminist lifestyle." Meeting strong, articulate women and listening to their visions of a future free of sexist inequity had awakened in me a ravenous craving to embrace my newfound allies, as well as a different kind of lust which had hitherto been dormant: *I wanted to fuck women.* This was a conscious desire I'd never so concisely formulated before. These women shunned traditional female roles, detested heterosexual convention. Certainly I was attracted to their ideas and aspirations, but primarily, as it turned out, because of how eminently more fuckable they made them seem to me. Needless to say, I jumped immediately and enthusiastically into bed with the first openly lesbian woman I met, no questions asked. Much personal grief and disappointment was to ensue, though: apparently, lesbians didn't fuck. Anything, *anything at all*, used to penetrate the vagina symbolized the phallus, evil tool of the patriarchy. Penetration emulated heterosexual inequality, I was told. I had found in my new girlfriend a soulmate, as well as a pathway to a deeper understanding of my womanly power, but I had yet to succeed in my baser quest for a proper fuck.

My girlfriend took me to pro-choice rallies, labor union protests, and lesbian bars. It was wonderful. My inner feminist began to

for more

emerge; but this did nothing to quell the emptiness I felt within. My male-identified/patriarchy-imposed impulse to fuck/get fucked would dissipate, I was told, and only then could I truly call myself a capital-L "Lesbian." In the meantime, my nightly pleas were met with consistent indignation. The abyss gaped.

It was with some trepidation that I attended the first meeting of my girlfriend's university women's group. I wasn't sure I was ready or committed enough to convene with women's studies majors and other feminist academics. My fears were not unfounded.

One woman, drinking some horrid-smelling brewed concoction, joyfully announced that she was bleeding into Mother Earth, and that her offensive beverage was an offering to the great menstrual spirit. This strange bulletin was welcomed by the group with veritable glee. Were we to feel jubilant about the onset of the monthly blood-fest I'd always found so loathsome? Or was this, as I theorized, an attempt to make a happy situation out of something miserable, simply because we had no choice in the matter?

Another woman, wearing a knotted Nicaraguan sweater-vest, re-affirmed her commitment to a lesbian lifestyle. Though she had yet to consummate her beliefs – she had never slept with another woman – she identified adamantly as a lesbian-feminist. Partners in a lesbian relationship are equals, thereby eliminating the heterosexual power struggle. Putting energy into each other empowers women as a whole, she said, and will ultimately render the patriarchal society unsustainable. All of which may very well be true, I postulated silently, although this politically motivated sexual preference was certainly not the motivation for my own constant urges.

Another woman, with a really, really bad haircut, vented her frustration at the pornography industry, testifying that these demeaning sexual depictions only exist to perpetuate the global oppression of women (Andrea Dworkin . . . blah, blah, blah . . .). But what about the portraits of naked women that graced the walls of our meeting room, I asked; weren't these pornography? I was informed that these were examples of woman-positive lesbian erotica, not pornography. I couldn't help but wonder if it wasn't all just different words for pictures of tits. I began to feel torn between knowing that I wanted to spend my time and energy with women, and suspecting that these very same women might leave me more confused and unfulfilled than when I began. Still, I resigned myself to the conviction that an alliance with this group was the only way to get laid.

Our meeting ended with the unanimous decision that we would form a special Women's Group Task Force to put pressure on the campus convenience store to stop selling pornography.

My best friend at the time was a sex-starved gay man, with whom I shared many common experiences besides our fruitless search for happiness. We were both the recipients of open hostility from the college jocks and other macho types in our residence. They hated him because they knew he wanted them. They hated me because they knew I didn't. He understood the dilemma my women friends were causing me, and had always been more than willing when I enlisted his help to buy my nudie magazines, lest my anti-porn feminist girlfriend catch me in the act. Now, with the availability of said literature in peril, I was faced with the prospect of either asking him to go downtown for my porn (a lot to ask of a friend), or ending my hypocrisy once and for all and accepting the fact that good feminists don't read jerk-off magazines.

My girlfriend had arranged, for our next women's group meeting, a private screening of Bonnie Klein's then-acclaimed anti-porn documentary *Not a Love Story*. I squirmed in my seat as I grew more and more aroused by the seedy, seamy images of the pustulant porn underground, images that were intended to sicken and disgust us.

The group engaged in lively discourse following the screening, evidently feeling validated and invigorated by this reproachful diatribe.

The woman drinking stinky tea agreed that the depiction of women as sex objects in the media was part of the great conspiracy to further the sexual subjugation of women. The one with the knotty sweater-vest lamented the fate of sex-trade workers, forced into a life of sleaze and prostitution by our misogynist society. The one with the bad haircut made some esoteric comment about hunters and gatherers that I didn't understand at all.

When my girlfriend called upon me for comment on the film, I declined as diplomatically as I knew how, but she insisted, determined as ever to bring me into the fold. My hesitant response was that some of the dirty bits kind of turned me on. I cited the specific example of the covertly shot illegal live sex show, during which a woman is on her back with her legs in the air while a man, pushing his partner's knees ever closer to her chest, soundly and deftly drills her with his huge, black cock. After the performance, the woman reveals to us during a backstage interview how she felt cheapened and degraded when she heard an audience member comment: "Fuck her, fuck that white bitch." This only added to the titillation, as far as I was concerned. A little hostility, a little humiliation, some dirty talk, and a lot of penetration – it sounded like a recipe for a pretty hot evening to me.

My girlfriend was mortified; her cohorts, scandalized. And it was at this precise moment I decided that this type of feminism is like a bunny rabbit: it seems like it might be a nice thing to have, but once you get it you realize it hates you and is full of crap. I was never to be invited to a women's group meeting, or to the bedroom of any of its members, ever again.

My university career ended shortly thereafter, but my feminist education continued. I discovered a more gratifying school of enlightenment. My new alma mater was a downtown full of women who talked trash and fucked like dogs, and whose behavior wasn't in the least created by any patriarchal institution, despite the women's group's claims to the contrary. I studied hard. I studied night and day, in public and in private, in groups and by myself; I studied up and down. I met women who reclaimed their right to sexual freedom – not a sexual freedom dictated to them by self-appointed women's rights despots, but one of their own design. I met women who shared much more than just my homosexual preference – they shared my proclivity for raunch and sleaze, an entirely different matter. I met women who were not only consumers of pornography but creators of it. I made a couple of (very bad) lesbian porn flicks myself. And while portraying girl scouts in bondage may have incensed others, such shamelessness was very much celebrated by my new circle of friends and fuck-buddies. We were proud to call ourselves bitches, sluts, and whores; we wore those labels like merit badges. We espoused the virtues of outrageous – even so-called obscene – sexual behavior. What could possibly be more empowering to women than giving ourselves permission to do whatever the hell we wanted to do with our bodies? Wanting to get fist-fucked, or fucked up the ass, or play-raped was fine. Not wanting it was fine too; but not wanting it – not wanting to even hear about it – because it offended some prudish sense of political propriety was just stupid.

I write comedy for the stage – plays, character sketches, short stand-up pieces – and to say I've borrowed materials from my encounters along the feminist journey would be an understatement. No one is immune from my creative exaggeration process – not the whining, anti-porn harridans who still exist (although in fewer numbers) and whom I still find detestable, nor the debauched pornographers who saved me from them.

My caricatures have ranged from Marie Benmergui's lover, an awkward, homely crone of a feminist who spews annoying, useless announcements to an audience of her sisters in struggle, to Francis, the main character of my *Dyke City* plays. Francis is a loud-mouthed, strap-on-dildo-wearing meat-eater who delights in telling humus-sucking, under-sexed feminists (like Marie Benmergui's lover) to "suck my cock." Fran is so obnoxious and politically incorrect that even hardcore bull dykes have been disconcerted when confronted by her.

Luckily, women learned to laugh at themselves somewhere along the way. If ball-scratching butches hadn't realized how strange and ridiculous they seem to the outside world (or even to most other lesbians), I'd be out of a job. And if strident women's rights devotees had remained as inflexible, repressed, and humorless as I tend to portray them, I'd be in even deeper shit.

I still wear men's underpants. They're just so damn comfortable! And I still maintain, through my lifestyle and through my work, that in order for women to command any sexual, social, or political power, we all need to talk dirty and fuck more, in whatever manner – approved-of or not – we feel compelled to. I maintain this even at the continuing risk of fueling dissent in our ranks.

IS THERE RADICALIZATION AFTER 40 ?

June Callwood

June Callwood is a journalist, broadcaster, and activist. A former columnist for the *Globe and Mail,* she is the author of numerous books, including *Trial Without Error, Twelve Weeks in Spring, Emma, Emotions,* and *The Sleepwalker.* She has founded and co-founded more than two dozen organizations that strive to change and improve social conditions. "Is There Radicalization After 40?" first appeared in *Maclean's* magazine in 1973, in slightly different form. Ms. Callwood lives in Toronto.

"Women's lib" was something of a novelty in the fall of 1972, when June Call-wood wrote this article. The Canadian Parliament had one woman member, and the esteemed editor of Chatelaine, *the country's most popular women's magazine, had shocked her colleagues by not quitting her job when her children were born. Looking back on those optimistic days before the "dark stuff" about abortion, family violence, and sexual abuse began to emerge, Callwood notes today that her 1972 self sounded like "a woman who has the world by the tail. I haven't felt like that in a long time. None of us has."*

THE SWISS GENIUS Jean Piaget says the learning process is, in part, integration and substitution. A two-year-old says *bastek* for *basket* until she reaches a state of readiness to make the change. When that happens her neural transistors make a note of it and, somewhere in the grainy grayness, her memory bank rings up *basket* for all time. The child experiences a flash of delight: getting it right feels good.

No one knows how a two-year-old prepares herself to accept new information, to give up the gluey comfort of a habit and push on. It's not likely therefore that I'm ever going to understand how I have moved so far and so fast into what is called Women's Lib. This past year in particular has been unnerving. I've had the feeling that for my forty-eight years I've been living on the other side of Alice's Looking-Glass, believing that Brainy Earth Woman was the ultimate female achievement, that the male-female relationship for the most part was founded on mutual respect, that the sexual position of common choice is an anthropomorphic truth: rampant male means gratified female.

Now I'm not certain what I believe. I was amazed to hear myself yell an obscenity during a recent blue-ribbon Conference on the Law in Ottawa, when a panel moderator thanked a woman who had just given an incisive speech by observing patronizingly, "When such an attractive woman talks to us, it is well to listen to what she has to say." And I'll never "Fly Carol" or "Fly Elaine" or Fly National, *ever*. And I'll never buy Dare cookies until the management agrees to pay its women employees the same wages it pays men for the same job. And I'll never eat in a restaurant where the waitresses are costumed to display their breasts and bottoms – are waiters ever hired on the basis of how well they are hung?

I feel as though I'm in a free fall through territory that looks familiar but is full of implications that aren't. This is the first winter of my life that I have been angry at newspaper pictures of women in bikinis in mammary poses on the beaches of Florida or Australia; I have never felt before that they were dehumanizing. For years I've been in the habit of using the copying machine in my publisher's office whenever I finish a book manuscript. Last spring, for the first time, I looked at the room where it stands: row on row of typists in a hollow square, all women, surrounded by sauntering men who belong to the cubicle offices on the perimeter. How is it possible that not one of those men, or any man, is not better suited to be a typist? How is it possible that not one of those women, or any woman, isn't capable of the better-paid tasks in the cubicles?

Formal weddings used to make me ache with the poignancy of all that stylized show of trust and commitment. The last one I attended, however, I kept wondering why the bride had that dumb curtain on her head, and why her father was leading her down the aisle to hand her over to the groom – *a man-to-man medieval transfer of property*. Why was her mother relegated to a seat in the bleachers? Why didn't the bride speak up when the clergyman asked, "Who gives this woman in holy matrimony?" – *is she a fully consenting adult or a warm Barbie doll?* And if premarital chastity is so wonderful that she has to be dressed in intact-hymen white, *why isn't the groom wearing white too?*

Also, I'm astonished at how I look lately. It's a minor but not insignificant indicator of what has happened to me. I had a moment of incredulity when I happened to get an objective glimpse of myself while lecturing to engineering students and faculty at McMaster University in Hamilton. I saw myself sitting on the lecture table, rather than standing demurely behind it, wearing stretch jeans, a turtleneck sweater, sandals, loose straight hair, and no makeup. Four years ago I was *arrested* looking better than that. When I was put in a cell, for failing to move along when so requested by a policeman at a protest rally, I was wearing a French import and a fresh hairdo, and my tears ruined eye makeup that had taken me five loving minutes to apply.

Piaget reports it's done by integration and substitution. I look behind me and there's nothing to see but a trackless lava slide. But there must be some way of comprehending how I got from there to here. Possibly a contributing factor to my bewilderment is that I am a second- and maybe a third-generation emancipated woman. My mother's mother scandalized her conservative French-Canadian village at the turn of the century by riding a galloping horse astride, and my mother has always worked. My father recruited her to help in his factory soon after I was born. When I was four my grandfather, a judge, recommended that I become a lawyer; he didn't tell me, so I didn't know, that law was a rare ambition for a woman. Nothing in my early experience therefore suggested that being female could impose any limitation.

I went to work at sixteen when a war-caused shortage of male reporters enabled me to be hired on the news side of a small-city daily paper as a reporter-photographer. I rarely covered women's events and was glad of it; the writing style required was beyond treacle, which seemed to suggest that women weren't very bright. I didn't believe it. I never thought of myself as a woman writer anyway. I was a writer with the cunning advantage of being female. I could flirt, cry, or wring my hands, whatever worked best. The only time it wasn't helpful was when I flew in a USAF B-17 and discovered the zippers in the air force flying suit issued me were inappropriately located.

After the war, when I was married and we had three children in the next six years, I found I could handily combine part-time magazine writing with nursing babies and learning what to do when the hollandaise curdles. When Betty Friedan came along in the early sixties, thumping the podium about women fulfilling themselves outside their homes, she struck me as a shrew who didn't know much about fulfillment.

Still the change in me was beginning. I think now it must have started years ago, when I was ecstatic to find myself pregnant with our fourth child. I had a revelation: all babies should be wanted. I was doing research in psychology and psychiatry at the time for a book I was writing on the human emotions, and in the scientific literature I found confirmation of what had been mainly intuition: a baby born where there isn't knowledge, tenderness, and time for her is forever blighted. She doesn't even grow to her physical potential, she doesn't have as good immunity to infection, her intelligence doesn't develop as it could, nor her self-esteem and ability to love. That information put me solidly in the abortion-on-demand camp, and some women in Ottawa were beginning a movement to change the law. I joined it.

Some years after that I began encountering studies that demonstrated babies not only require fondling and respect but have needs for an environment that provides variety and stimulation. Clearly mothers should have that sort of information, so I began pushing for child-care education in the schools. Almost as an afterthought I proposed, at an Ontario-wide conference called "The Troubled Child," that both males and females should be instructed in the needs of children and preferably should be exposed to an actual nursery or day-care center. That, and studies which established that two- and three- and four-year-olds benefit greatly from being able to play together, made me an enthusiastic advocate of day care as a child's right.

I had backed into Women's Lib issues without noticing. *They* were proposing abortion and day care in order to permit women to plan their lives with the same continuity as men do, without pausing for a mind-dissolving fifteen years of child-tending. *I* was brimming with the joys of enlightened motherhood. I must have given them a frightful pain, and they dismayed me. But we were stuck with one another: our goals were the same.

My editor at Doubleday in New York, Lisa Drew, began writing "Ms." on her letters to me. The feminist Kate Millett had just written a grumpy Doubleday book, *Sexual Politics*, and the office was full of The Movement. Ms. made perfect sense from the moment I first saw it. Eventually society will drop the whole clumsy, often inaccurate, and usually redundant apparatus of Mr., Mrs., Miss, and Ms., but in the meantime Ms. answers the problem of a woman's marital status being written on her forehead while a man's is not.

The Canadian Civil Liberties Association sent me a notice of an executive committee meeting. My name has been on the list of officers printed on CCLA stationery for the past eight years but for the first time something about it jumped out at me. "How come," I demanded when I got to the meeting, "that it reads 'Miss June Callwood' and 'Mrs. Barbara Frum'? How come it doesn't read 'Dalton Camp (Married)' and 'Alan Borovoy (Single)'?"

Borovoy, the association's general counsel, dragged his hand down his face and groaned, "You've gone Women's Lib!"

I was indignant. "I have not! It's a question of relevancy, that's all."

I collaborated with a lawyer, Marvin A. Zuker, on a small book called *Canadian Women and the Law*. Sandra Precop reviewed it in the

Windsor Star and commented on its "screaming 'discrimination' from cover to cover." That hadn't been the original intention. We planned to produce a simple, readable guide on the rights and responsibilities of women under the law. Zuker has an academic mind, meticulous and detached, and he provided the legal research. When I saw it, my contribution to the book became a howl from the heart. In some cases, as with alimony and the custody of children, the law discriminates against men, but the effect of most of the laws concerning women is to flatten them. It's done out of gallantry: women are frail, they can't cope, they need protection. Kindly meant or not, the consequence is that women ride in the back of the bus. Female dependency, which can become female despair, is built into the system.

I still didn't know anyone in the Women's Lib movement but I began to wish they would talk more about jobs and less about their dear little uteruses. The rationale, obviously, is that a woman cannot compete for responsible positions without being able to control her own procreation. But the attraction of childbearing for some women is that it offers the only sense of accomplishment they'll ever know. The baby becomes the justification of the mother's whole life, which can be soul-breaking for both. Women should have a choice or two, besides motherhood.

I was becoming political. For eight months I had been writing then prime minister Pierre Trudeau asking him to consider a Royal Commission on the Needs of Children or, at least, a Prime Minister's Conference similar to the White House Conference on Children that is mandatory in the United States every ten years. He almost never replied, even when I attempted to make the letters humorous, which is a neat trick to pull off when you are trying to tell someone that a lot of children are suffering.

I came to the conclusion that the difficulty must be the ratio of the sexes in Parliament: at that time 263 men and one valiant woman. If there were more women, maybe we wouldn't have conditions like those in Montreal slum areas where a survey found half the schoolchildren weakened by malnutrition. Maybe we would, but it seemed worth a try.

The Progressive Conservatives, the New Democratic Party, and the Liberals, in that order, asked me to be a federal candidate. I pictured the scene in the backrooms: cigar smoke curling up, ties loosened, ice melting in the glasses: "Hey, *Chatelaine* says we need more women candidates this time. *Does anyone know a woman?*" (*Chatelaine* had published in October 1971 a tightly documented, strongly worded blast against the parties' sexist attitudes.)

I finally decided against running for any party, giving as my reason the unlikelihood that I could persuade any caucus to make the lives of babies the top government priority and the certainty that I would turn myself into a caricature of a self-anointed revivalist by trying.

All this was true, but the deeper truth that I omitted has to do with my family. Even on my best days I operate with less confidence than I need. The supportive friendship of my daughters and sons, and especially of my husband, enables me to overcome this and feel frisky and invincible. Because of the family bond, I am free of the fear of failure or fall from dignity that immobilizes many people; I am absolutely safe. To become a politician, and be separated from them, would be to tinker with a miracle.

About that time some women in Toronto, aroused by the *Chatelaine* article, were pondering the dearth of women in political life. They made some telephone calls, from which emerged a meeting. About forty of us collected in a church basement, mostly strangers to one another, a cross-section of ages and styles. The tone was restrained and polite as we exchanged views. We agreed on a name – Women for Political Action – and some decisions that were born of a mistrust of structure: we wouldn't have a constitution, we wouldn't become a national movement, we wouldn't have formal memberships, or an executive, or a permanent chairperson. (*Chairperson*, I thought, exasperated; it gets absurd: repairperson? clergyperson? landperson?)

We continued to meet, though the chaos produced by the egalitarian approach almost swamped us. Hundreds of women came and went, and those who went departed mainly because of the decision to run two women as Independent candidates in the federal election, a historic first born of disillusionment. We kept being told, mainly by women, that we were naive at best and destructive to the cause at worst to be working outside the system.

Outside the system! There is nothing more hoary with tradition in the evolution of democracy in Canada than for people who feel themselves powerless and shut out of decision-making to get together to acquire clout. Before we even had responsible government, indignation and frustration created the nineteenth-century Reform Party. In the early twenties aroused farmers elected sixty-five of themselves to the House of Commons within a year of organizing. The process goes that way: parties solidify when they are in power in order to be reassuring, eventually the desirable stability becomes undesirable stagnancy and alienation, which spends what little energy it has on defending itself. A new force comes along and for a flashy few minutes there is responsiveness and vitality again.

I had a vision of women across the country coming spontaneously and simultaneously to a sense of common cause and electing a ferocious dozen or so to Ottawa. Oh well. Maybe when the next federal election rolls around, women shut out in the last one will either run on the simple ticket *Woman* or devise new tactics.

Rosemary Brown, who was to become a member of the legislature in British Columbia, described an alternative route for women in politics during a "Strategy for Change" Conference sponsored by the National Action Committee on the Status of Women in Canada. She recommended that women select a strong riding association, one that usually gets its candidate elected, and join it in droves. They should keep a low profile, contentedly stuffing envelopes, until it is time to choose a candidate or elect an executive. Then they surface, pack the meeting, and put women in power.

Women for Political Action didn't have the luxury of time, even if we had trusted the parties to pay attention to women within their ranks, which we didn't. We concentrated on campaign strategy, on how to elect two women to the House of Commons on a budget of almost nothing. The meetings drew an ill-sorted group of women: some young and wearing jeans and army boots, some white-haired with their knitting, some from factories, some matrons in hats. There were moments when we seemed to be appreciating one another in a wave of oneness that was endearing and enlarging. In consciousness-raising groups, I'm told, women feel similar bonds of shared experience so intensely that they weep. The surprise in the Women's Lib Cracker Jack box is liking women better, from which flows liking one's self more.

I still didn't feel that I was really a part of Women's Lib. One major divergence was my feeling that women have inviolable responsibility for the raising of their children, whether it means suspending research worthy of a Nobel Prize or quitting the curling club. I changed my mind by imperceptible degrees in the weeks after a casual conversation with Charlotte Sykes. She's a longtime feminist who sometimes wears a button, "UPPITY WOMEN UNITE." We met while working together to raise money for some low-income tenants to fight a developer who wanted their houses. I had located someone in an advertising agency who was willing to help.

"The trouble is that his schedule is jammed right now," I explained to her one day. "Something truly terrible has happened. His wife has left him with two small children and he's trying to hold his job and take care of them at the same time."

There was an unaccountable silence. It stretched on. Then Sykes said quietly, "Would Friday noon be all right?"

From time to time after that I thought about the silence. I had sensed disagreement, but how could anyone approve of children being in agony over a mother's rejection? I tried to reason it out. If the mother left, presumably her attachment to the children was slight. The children then were being deprived not of someone caring but of someone disinterested; it's still a loss, but maybe not a crippling one. If the father changed his priorities, if he was warm, if the housekeeper was affectionate, the children might be much better off than with a mother longing to be free.

I reviewed the literature on the needs of infants and small children. It says that they must have love, consistency, proper food, touching, stimulation – but nowhere does it say that these essentials can be provided only by the biological mother. In fact, the pioneer in studies of infants, Dr. John Bowlby, now refers to the tending adult by the neutral word "care-taker," while a Toronto psychologist investigating day care is using the term "care-giver." In other words, anyone of any adult age or sex who has the time, knowledge, intelligence, and inclination to care tenderly for a baby is perfectly suited to do so. My prejudice had always been that only mothers can mother, that all mothers must mother, and I suddenly realized I'd been wrong.

I will never come to agree, however, with that aspect of Women's Lib which is anti-men. There's no improvement in the human condition in replacing discrimination against women with discrimination against men. Besides, men have paid a grim price for their monopoly on power: their humanity. When sex stereotyping eventually stops, men will be the greater beneficiaries. Women will get the right to achievement, which may give them ulcers, but men will get something better – empathy, intuition, compassion, colors.

It's women, anyway, who most loudly insist that female helplessness is adorable and female accomplishment is deviant behavior. We have made it come true by believing that nonsense.

So here I am, Women's Lib. How did I get here? *And what took me so long?*

THE *Bride* OF CHRIST

PAMELA DES BARRES

||||||||||||||||||||||||||

Pamela Des Barres

is a journalist, editor, and writer who is best known for two memoirs:
I'm with the Band (1987) and *Take Another Little Piece of My Heart* (1992).
Both works vividly chronicle her days as part of the American music scene
in the sixties and seventies and her relationships with, among others,
Jim Morrison, Jimmy Page, Waylon Jennings, and Mick Jagger. She was
a member of the groundbreaking group The GTOs, the all-girl band
produced by Frank Zappa. She lives in California, where she is
at work on a novel about the life of Mary Magdalene.

▼

The Bride of Christ

If I had been Mary Magdalene
I would have touched my lips
to the hem of His garment
Nothing could have stopped me from
Stroking His immaculate thigh
Baring my quivering soul
to this God made flesh –
this Light dipped in hell
Come to secure my soul
From the clutches
Of the unholy temple
Made holy by His caress.

MARY MAGDALENE was not a whore. She was not somebody who needed to be redeemed, delivered, saved, or rescued. She was not an adulteress, a "fallen woman," or an unholy sinner, scooped from the pit of lasciviousness by a meek and forgiving savior. While women were forbidden to recite religious lessons in public, and were seated apart from the men in the synagogue, Magdalene was an independent woman who did exactly what she wanted to do – against all odds. She left her family and friends, her culture and religion to walk beside – not to follow – a rebellious, outspoken teacher called Jesus.

Along with the original fallen woman, the evil Eve (when she enticed the flawless Adam with the apple/fig, they noticed their nakedness, the serpent/Satan arrived, and therefore human sexuality was *sinful*), Mary Magdalene's fictitious shame has put women "in their place" for centuries. By the fourth century, celibacy was encouraged by the church, and at the end of the sixth century, Pope Gregory had lumped Mary Magdalene in with two other sinful females, thus turning Christ's beloved into a repenting prostitute. Shame, shame, shame.

Discovered in Cairo in 1896, fragments of

the Gnostic Gospel of Mary were finally published in 1955. Most likely written in the late first or early second century, the Gospel of Mary shakes up the idea that early Christian women were subservient slaves, acquiescing to their men. Or perhaps Magdalene was a rare bird in the desert. It is obvious from the text that Mary was a leader in Jesus' growing movement, a woman with great spiritual power, who actually took over the role of teacher to the disciples when Jesus was tending to other needy souls. Sometimes she needed to *explain* to the fellows what Jesus had really meant, and they weren't amused. Sometimes they just didn't get it.

When Jesus chose to appear to Mary after being crucified, she reported the vision to the disciples. Peter doubted her, but Levi argued: "If the Savior considered her to be worthy, who are you to disregard her? For He knew her completely and loved her devotedly." The Coptic gospels are even more revealing. Peter again: "Did he then speak with a woman in private without our knowing about it? Are we to turn around and listen to her? Did he choose her over us?" The answer was even more succinct: "Assuredly the Savior's knowledge of her is completely reliable. Because of this He loved her more than He loved us."

The Gospel of Philip described Magdalene as the "companion" of Jesus, and when one of the disciples asked why he "used to kiss her often on her mouth," Jesus responded, "Because I kiss her often on her mouth." Such a cool answer. The Greek word *koinonos* used to depict Magdalene is usually translated as "companion," but is more correctly translated as "partner" or "consort" – a woman with whom a man has sexual relations. Who knows? Nowhere in the Bible does it state otherwise. When I was in Israel, my tour guide, a biblical scholar, told me that it was very likely that Magdalene and Jesus were lovers.

This startling possibility has been a revelation to me. When I was the tender baby-age of eight years old, I found myself walking down the center aisle at the Hume Lake Camp Church, scared to pieces, trembling with shame, weaving between the pews, ready to hurl my wicked girlish sins at the feet of the meek and mild Master, to humble myself in the blinding blaze of His halo. All around me, tear-stained faces urged me forward. Each step hurt. I knew how Jesus felt as He carried His cross through the jeering throngs because my Lord's crown of thorns was poking through my sneakers. When I finally reached the solemn minister I got down on my scabby knees to beg sweet Jesus to *please* forgive me for . . . for what? What kind of unholy sins could I have committed in my meager eight years on the planet? I couldn't even tell a lie. But still, Jesus said we were all born sinners, didn't He? (He never said that, actually – many words have been put into His mouth in the name of guilt. "Thou shalt not" wasn't in His vocabulary.) If he could save the naughty temptress Mary Magdalene from a life of depravity, just think what He could do for me! I looked into the glare of the minister's glasses and told him I was ready to receive Christ as my savior. (I was secretly glad I wasn't in a Catholic church where you had to "eat His body and drink His blood." Yikes.) It was over almost before it began. The freaked-out eight-year-old was Born Again. People cheered, they clapped and wept, but I didn't feel any different. I felt like I had been coerced. Then I felt guilty for feeling that way and instantly begged forgiveness. This went on for years.

According to my various pastors, *fornication* was a major sin. I had always thought that fornication meant having sex. During the time of the Bible, it actually meant adultery – sex with someone who was married to someone else. And the Complete Gospels translates the word *fornication* as: "Adulterous union with the flesh" (putting the flesh before the spirit – an entirely different meaning). Meanwhile, I entered my pubescence during the freewheeling free-love sixties and was fraught with guilt every time I came. And with rock stars yet! I tortured myself for enjoying the pleasures of the flesh, asking Jesus (whom I had actually come to resent, truth be told – which of course, caused me great and thunderous guilt) why, why, *why*, if sex was so damn sinful, did it feel so fucking good? It also had the potential of creating life. Shouldn't it be an ecstatic experience? He never gave me a good answer, so I kept on throbbing along with Mick Jagger and Jimmy Page, and saved my repenting for later. It ate me up.

I tortured myself into severe migraines, which I believed were created by sin (I now know they were created by my belief that I somehow deserved to be punished). My sweet Lord was frowning on me. I could feel it. Still, I flounced around in see-through lace tablecloths under the summer love-in sun, popped my birth control pills on the Sunset Strip for all to see (my own version of feminism), dropped acid, and danced onstage with the Mothers of Invention, storing up the guilt for a rainy day. I braved some severe storms.

The acid helped. When I saw the molecules of life pulsating in the seemingly empty air, I also saw through some of the illusory trumped-up fraud and began to question the hallowed pages of the Bible, seeking passages that might acquit me. Hopefully the ones in red, spoken by the Lord himself. "If God so clothe the grass, which is today in the field, and tomorrow is cast into the oven; how much more will he clothe you, oh ye of little faith?" He had indeed provided me with a lovely little lace tablecloth! "There is joy in the presence of the angels of God over one sinner that repenteth." But what was sin, anyway? And how did one repent? Being Born Again hadn't done a damn thing for me. According to the Complete Gospels, sin means "joining things that do not belong together, specifically the spiritual nature of the Good with material nature." And in my concentrated study of the Word of God, I didn't find one single passage that led me to believe that Mary Magdalene was a whore.

Jesus said that the lion and the lamb must learn to lie down together. The soul and the body have to make friends to get through this intense journey. It took me years of study and deep pondering to have sex without any hint of guilt. I have come (ha!) to realize that orgasm is bliss – the closest most people ever come to unity with God.

Mary Magdalene was not someone who needed to be redeemed, delivered, saved, or rescued, and neither am I. The love and gratitude I feel for my sister in spirit – who dared to walk that heady, joyous, and difficult path alongside the greatest teacher the world has ever known – is profound. The bride of Christ braved the storm, and so can I.

Actually, I can do better than *brave* the storm; I can make love during a typhoon, have wild sex in a blizzard. I can come buckets in a hailstorm.

And Jesus doesn't mind.

Artist **Jenny Holzer's** medium is language: her work has appeared on
T-shirts, stickers, movie marquees, billboards, electronic signs, television,
the Internet, and, most recently, laser and xenon
projections.
She has cre-
ated word-based installations at museums and
in public locations worldwide, and her style has
been described as
ranging from the
coolly logical to the explosively mad. Holzer
was the first woman to rep-
resent the United
States at the Venice Biennale.
She lives in New York.

M O M E N T S

Nawal El-Saadawi is an award-winning novelist, a psychiatrist, and an activist whose works on the situation of women in Arab society have been translated into several languages. Imprisoned in Cairo in the early 1980s for her political writing and involvement with Arab women's organizations, her name remains on an extremist group's death list. Now based in Cairo, Nawal El-Saadawi has received honorary degrees from the University of York in Britain and the University of Illinois at Chicago; she has taught at the University Center for International Studies at Duke University in Durham, North Carolina.

N A W A L
E L - S A A D A W I

I WAS SEVEN YEARS OLD when the first experiences of my life began to filter through my consciousness, sometimes like the dawn emerging slowly out of the darkness, sometimes like lightning flashes illuminating the sky.

But my memory tells me that these were not the first moments of illumination in my life. The day I was born I remember opening my eyes as I slipped out into the world and seeing faces that stared at me without a smile. Like a distant dream I can see them to this day.

I did not know why my birth was not a source of happiness and joy to my mother

and father and to the other women and men in the family. But the moment came like a flash of light when I understood the reason: I was a girl, not a boy. I was crawling on the floor, not knowing then how to stand or walk or talk. I saw the eyes around me fastened on the area between my thighs and understood there was something missing, the name of which I had not learned as yet, even though I knew what it looked like. I had seen it hanging between my brother's thighs, with a thin stream of water shooting out of it. When the women spotted it, they would gleam with pride and happiness and the yoo-yoos shrilled from deep in their throats.

Such moments of understanding succeeded one another through the days and months. Every instant of light brought with it a thrust of pain that stabbed into my heart. So I learned that every moment of knowledge brings with it a moment of pain and that somehow the two are always linked.

When I reached the age of seven, my father started to teach me how to pray. My father used to pray without covering his head. My brother, who was one year older than I was, did the same. But when I began to pray, my father said, "Nawal, you must cover up your head when you pray." I asked my father why, and his answer was, "When you pray you are standing before Allah [God] and must give Him all respect." So I said, "Is covering the head an indication of respect?" and he answered, "Yes, of course. You cannot stand in front of God with no cover on your head."

"But then, Father, why do you pray to God without a cover on your head? Why does my brother bare his head when he prays to God? Do both of you have no respect for God?"

My father was silent for a moment. It seemed as though he had to find an answer to my question, needed to think it out. I realized that my father was taken aback, searching for an answer, pondering the difference between the head of a man and that of a woman, why a woman should be obliged to cover her head during prayer, whereas the head of the man could remain bare, and what was the relation between respect and the covering of the head.

My father's voice faltered when he answered me: the hair of women is *awra* (shameful) and should not be seen, but the hair of men is not.

I did not understand what the word *awra* meant. My father tried to explain it to me. He said *awra* means the shameful parts of the body – such as the breast or thigh – which have to be covered so that the eyes of others cannot see them. If exposed, made visible, it would lead to corruption, to seduction, to immoral behavior.

At seven, my mind could accept that the reproductive organs of men and women should be hidden by their clothes and that the breasts and the belly and the thighs should not be exposed. But why should the head of a woman be considered shameful? That was something my mind could not assimilate. Besides, what was the difference between the head of a woman and that of a man?

My father reached in vain for a clear difference between them. The only answer he could give was that the hair of men was short and unattractive, whereas that of women was long and flowing, full of seductive appeal. But my father's reasoning did not convince me, especially where praying was concerned, since no one saw me as I prayed. It was only God who would see my hair, and surely God was not like any man in the street to be seduced.

However, I went to the hairdresser and had my hair cut short like my brother, and began to pray like him without covering my head. But when my father saw this, he insisted that I should still cover my head or else all my prayers would be to no avail. So I questioned my father again. This time he said that these were the rules laid down by Allah and Allah's orders had to be obeyed without discussion. I began to wonder how I could obey orders that were not convincing to me. God was supposed to be a symbol of reason and logic with no faults in what He said. We could accept incomplete reasoning or illogical thought from human beings, but God was perfect and there could be no fault with His reasoning or contradictions in what He orders us to do.

My father failed to convince me of the difference between my head and that of my brother. My hair was as short as his and there could be no other difference between us than that between the brains each of us carried in the skull.

Was there any difference between my brain and his? Yes, there certainly was. I was brilliant at school, passed my exams with distinction, whereas my brother kept failing all the time. Everyone said I was more intelligent than him. Why then should I cover my head in shame, whereas my brother went around with an uncovered head and without the slightest feeling of shame? Reason seemed to say that the less intelligent should be the one who feels shame.

So from the age of seven I started to refuse, to disobey all orders that did not convince me. My father was the one who encouraged me to use my brain in dealing with whatever I had to face. Yet, when it came to God and matters like covering my head during prayers he wanted me to stop thinking. But my brain refused to work this way, to think for one moment and to stop thinking the next.

At the age of nine, I awoke one morning and found blood in my knickers. I was so scared. I knew nothing about menstruation. I was told that it was a kind of punishment meted out to women and that it caused their bodies to be defiled. For Allah said in the Holy Koran, "If they question you about menstruation, say it is a punishment [aza] that causes women to be unclean. Therefore, keep away from them during their periods until they are purified." My grandmother explained to me that the blood of the menses was "impure," that it was foul, corrupt blood, that during her period a girl should not touch the Koran, or read, or pray. It was as though her tongue became foul, her hands unclean. A person who had done his or her ablutions would be defiled by shaking hands with her.

I would wash my body over and over, from the top of my head down to my toes, wash my hands with hot water and soap time after time, but somehow the uncleanliness would continue to cling to my body like some evil spirit until my period was over.

I was seized by a kind of "washing neurosis," driven by a desire to cleanse myself of this impure menstruation. In the primary school which I attended in the district town of Menouf, all the girls in my class were affected by the same neurosis. Most of them were Muslims, but some of them were Copts (Christians) or Jews. My Jewish friend Sarah was the most neurotic of all. In the Old Testament there is a verse which says, "During the time of her menses a woman is unclean for seven days. Everything holy is not to be touched by her, until she is completely pure. If a woman becomes pregnant and gives birth to a male she will be purified after thirty-three days. If she gives birth to a female, she does not become pure except after sixty-six days. She who completes her day of purification should sacrifice a sheep and a pigeon or dove and offer it to God, who will forgive her for her sins and purify her from the uncleanliness of her blood."

As young girls we began to ask ourselves questions. Why was the blood in our bodies unclean? Why did the uncleanliness after the birth of a female child last twice the time it did after the birth of a male? Why should a woman offer a sheep and a pigeon or a dove in order to have herself absolved from her sins and be purified? What does a poor woman do if she does not have a sheep or a pigeon or a dove to sacrifice, and will she remain unclean in the eyes of her God because she is poor?

I felt a little exalted because in the Koran God had not asked for the sacrifice of a sheep or a pigeon or a dove. I began to feel pity for Sarah and other Jewish girls. However, this feeling of exaltation evaporated as soon as my father told me that a Muslim must believe in the three Holy Books – the Old Testament, the New Testament, and the Koran – since they were all God's books.

I lived long moments of humiliation and shame whenever my period arrived. But deep inside, I felt that my blood was as sacred, clean, and precious as the blood of my brother. I was more intelligent than he was, passed my exams at school with distinction, so why was my blood impure? I asked God: Why? God did not answer. My father could not answer. My teacher in school said, "This is God's will. Menstrual blood has been a punishment by God since Eve's sin." What was Eve's sin? I asked the teacher, who replied that Eve had eaten from the Tree of

Knowledge. But why was it a sin to eat from the Tree of Knowledge? As a child I believed that knowledge was a positive thing. The teacher told our class that we should seek knowledge as much as we could. I then asked if God would punish me for seeking knowledge in school. The teacher could not answer my questions. His silence gave me the courage to continue asking and to insist on solving this paradox.

God seemed unfair for punishing me because I loved knowledge. God seemed unfair for punishing Eve because she ate from the Tree of Knowledge: How could that knowledge be a sin?

These first questions that I asked myself (and that nobody answered) were the most important of my life. They were the ones that clicked open the door and allowed in the first flashes of light.

sacred revela

tions

of " **the**

debra

oren

stein

DEBRA

is a seventh-generation rabbi and an actress who writes and speaks extensively on spirituality and gender studies. A senior fellow of the Wilstein Institute

ORENSTEIN

of Jewish Policy Studies and an instructor at the University of Judaism in Los Angeles, she is also a popular scholar-in-residence and guest lecturer throughout North America. Her latest books are *Lifecycles 1: Jewish Women on Life Passages and Personal Milestones* and *Lifecycles 2: Jewish Women on Biblical Themes in Contemporary Life* (co-edited with Jane Litman).

click"

I WAS WITH MY MOTHER in a dark and confusing place. Doctors, my father, various authoritative males were telling her to "stop being hysterical." "Nothing's wrong. Your daughter is not coming." But I *was* coming, I was *here*, and I hardly knew what to do. Come out? Hide out? I didn't want to make them *or* my mother wrong. It felt like she was in danger. My mother, my role model, the good, sometimes resentful girl, went home, denying what she knew. But she had been right. I was half with her, half without her. Perhaps I *was* her. I felt myself pushed inexorably forward, ambivalent.

No, this isn't a dream. It's the story of my birth – my first "click." I don't tell it as I remember it; I *don't* remember it. And I don't tell it as it's been passed down to me. That version is a funny, silly Marx Brothers–style farce with a happy ending.

The version I tell now is another selection from the multiplicity of narratives and meaning. It is today's snapshot of a moving, evolving etiology: the story of how I, and perhaps of how Woman, was born. Not from a rib (Woman from man's body), but rather from a struggle (Woman from man's society). It has its own truth – somber, complex, reflecting my mother's relationship to a male-dominated world and presaging my own.

APPARENTLY a medical intern forgot to plug in some monitor, and my mother was told she wasn't in labor. "I think this is it," she said. "This *is* my second child." But she was ordered home and she went. According to my maternal grandmother, my mother finally believed her own body when, in great pain, she went to the bathroom at home to try to relieve the pressure and noticed that my head was in the toilet. This is a source of some controversy, as my mother denies that part of the story. My father, a rabbi who has been known to feel squeamish at the sight of blood, "delivered" me at home just twenty minutes after they returned from the hospital, freeing a twisted ankle that held me in the birth canal. He followed directions given over the phone by an emergency room doctor who was almost as dismayed by the situation as he. Meanwhile, my grandmother went to a public phone and called one ambulance service after another, failing each time to give the address. At some point my father asked her why she was so frantic. "Because you're so calm," she replied. The push-me pull-you of gender relations and family dynamics.

After my mother was proven "right," after I made the decision to be born, I was quiet. My father relates that in the first seconds after birth my eyes were open; I was looking around the room curiously, taking in the strange and interesting face in front of me – his. (According to the doctors of that era, babies couldn't see at birth; a few months after I was born, my father read in a news report that the medical establishment had changed its collective mind. He likes to think that he made the discovery. I like to think that I defied the doctors on my mother's behalf.)

My mother said, "Hit her." My father said, "We are communing. I am having a nice conversation with my daughter." My mother said, "Hit her." My father said, "I will not." My mother said, "Hit her. She's not crying. She's not breathing. You've got to clear the lungs." My father said, "She's breathing. We're talking here." My mother said, "Hit her, for God's sake." And my father did. He held me upside-down by one ankle (the one he dislodged?), and he gave me a *pach* – Yiddish for a smack on the rump. He reports that I looked at him with an expression of betrayal that said, "How could you do that? I trusted you." And then I cried, loudly, to prove that I was hurt and therefore breathing.

In the hospital (the second time, postpartum), I stayed with my mother, as I was too unsterile to be in the nursery with the other babies. Periodically, a doctor or nurse would walk in and ask, "Did she get drops in the eyes just after birth?" "Did you notice anything about the skin?" "Did anyone look at that ankle?" "No? Well, never mind. I'm sure it's not important."

The jumbled, confused messages of my first click were conveyed before I could either understand or rebel: You did it wrong. You are indecisive. You are hysterical. The stakes are always life and death. Nobody listens – especially not men. You don't know your own body. It isn't safe to come out. Do; don't; do. Men don't want you to be born. Women do, though they don't always know how to defend you or themselves. You and your mother are not quite separable. Mothers are right, fearful, and require protection; they cede their authority to everyone but their children.

Another message: Despite it all, you did it.

My mother read this new version of the story and offered another perspective: It was the two of us against the world. We were the ones who knew what we were doing. And my father's calm was a great blessing. Together, he and my mother were in charge of this birth in a way they were not for their hospital-born babies. I was so quiet at birth, she imagined, because of the tranquility in their bedroom.

Ah, mothers.

IN MY THIRTIETH YEAR, I took a wonderful interfaith seminar. The culminating exercise was a simple one. Break into groups of four, take about an hour each to ask for whatever you want. When it is your turn, let the others give it to you. When you are serving someone else, give with all your heart. The exercise was inspired by a woman who said she felt a void in her life because she had never been baptized as a child. The leader decided, "Then let the group go back and do it for you now. Have your baptism exactly as you always wanted it."

I asked to be rebirthed. I didn't give very clear directions. I just told them about my birth, and said I wanted something more peaceful and welcoming. I had a "bad" group. These were near strangers, no one I had worked with before, no one with whom I had developed a trust. They were, of course, perfect.

There was only one man. He played my father. He told me that he was excited to have me there, that everyone was prepared and ready for me, that it was safe to come out. One of the two women took on a role none of us planned or was conscious of. I could not name it until afterward. She was a healing, beatific presence. Her voice was comfort itself, and, even with my eyes closed, she was all Light. She represented for me Shekhinah – the close-dwelling, feminine presence of God – said by the ancient rabbis to be a partner with father and mother in every act of proCreation. The other woman took the role of mother, telling me, "We so want a baby! We are so glad to have you here!" All three of them hugged me, as one would hug a baby. On the written page, it all sounds so foolish and New Age–juvenile. It was an extraordinary and, strangely, a subtle experience.

Something struck me as out of place, uncomfortable. With my group's support, against the messages of my "real" birth experience and my socialization as a woman, I stopped them. I corrected them; I told them it wasn't exactly what I wanted. I requested of my "mother": "Don't say you want a baby. Say you want a girl."

My parents love me, but I have always sensed that they, and especially my father, hoped for a boy. They *had* a girl, my older sister. Boys carry on your name and play sports and chess and do music and magic tricks and become rabbis. In my rabbinic family, these are – or were – "boys' things."

My seminar "mother" told me she wanted a girl, and my "father" and "Shekhinah" chimed in. I was meant to be a girl and blessed as one.

Afterward, we talked. My "father" confessed that, as an American man of German extraction, he had always felt guilty about the Germans' role in the Holocaust and was, with respect to Jews, ashamed of his heritage. He was grateful for the liberating opportunity to sire a Jew – and a rabbi, no less! A burden was lifted from him. The woman who had embodied Shekhinah said that she had always considered herself to be spiritually deficient. To see herself through my eyes and the eyes of others in the group was a gift. Truly, she shone. My "mother" told me that her real-life daughter had gone through an extended period, inappropriate to her age, of throwing tantrums. The problem was bad enough that the mother consulted a therapist. In the course of her counseling, she admitted that she had wanted a boy and was both disappointed with her daughter and furious with herself for having such a vile, sexist, unmaternal sentiment. The therapist helped her understand and forgive herself for wanting a son. When, after a short time, the mourning was done and the guilt was cleared, she was able to see that her love for this little girl was as strong and irreplaceable as the girl herself. Her daughter abruptly stopped throwing tantrums. In asking this mom to voice how much she wanted a girl, I unknowingly created a rebirth for her as well as for me.

And some part of me had always been worried that my birth was a burden.

I COULD RELATE many stories of sexism, of mistreatment, of sexual discrimination and harassment. As a woman in the rabbinate, a field of religious leadership closed to women for millennia, maybe I have had more click experiences than my share. The negative incidents shock me into awareness and have sometimes motivated me to make major changes. But they cannot compare in raw power to the rarer affirmations, to the occasions when, as at that seminar, I realized how right and lucky and miraculous it is to be exactly who I am. "Blessed are You, God, Ruler of the universe, who has made me a woman."[1]

Blessings often last where curses fade. The memory of an early domineering and sexist boyfriend lingers. I can still recall the ways he tried to control me. The kinds of wounds he inflicted go deep – deep enough to inspire rebellion. Yet his influence on my life and my feminism cannot compare to that of another young man I met during a school vacation. His family hosted mine for a few days when we traveled abroad. A virtual stranger, he treated me with kindness and as an absolute equal, reminding me of what was – or should be – normal. A loud click went off in my head when he didn't mock what I cared about (we happened to be talking about the Bible), but instead expressed his own interests and enthusiasm. I wonder what would have happened if I hadn't met

1. Orthodox Jewish men offer a traditional blessing each morning, "Blessed are You, God, Ruler of the universe, who has not made me a woman." Orthodox women say, "Blessed are You, God, Ruler of the universe, who has made me according to Your will." All non-Orthodox Jews say instead, "Blessed are You, God, Ruler of the universe, who has created me in Your image."

him or a young man like him. I never dated him. I spent a grand total of ten or twelve hours with him. But he unknowingly gave me the hope, insight, and courage to break up with a boyfriend I might well have married otherwise. In light of the contrast, I understood how unacceptable and unnecessary it was to be treated as I had been. Love, gender relations, didn't have to "cost" me or degrade me.

Positive experiences nurture the "born feminist" in me – the part of me that experiences being female as normal and central, not other and marginal; the part of me that becomes indignant over injustice; the part of me that read feminist literature at age fifteen and said, "Of course." Yes, identity – even feminist identity – is socially constructed. Yes, I internalized sexism even as I rebelled against it. Yes, I have been shaped by innumerable outside influences – from family and school to the Jewish tradition and the media. But I also believe there is something innate that takes in and resonates with all my experiences. I would call that something a soul, a feminist soul.

I owe, my soul owes, a lot to my siblings. My younger brother and I shared a bathroom growing up. One day, when he left the toilet seat up, it suddenly struck me as odd that he stood up to urinate. I asked him in all innocence and egocentrism, "Isn't it weird being a boy?" "No, I like it," he replied. "But isn't it weird being a girl?" "No," I told him. "I like it, too." We each walked away relieved and enlightened. Relating to a brother with whom I share so much, I realized – not just during that one exchange, but over the last few decades – how silly it is to develop strictures and assumptions around such trivial questions as who stands up to pee. I learned a feminist and joyous acceptance of diversity from my "weird" brother. I found in him a shining example of a truly good and trustworthy man.

If my brother taught me to distance myself from sex-role divisions, my sister pointed to their persistent social power. She helped to radicalize the family – my father and brother, I am proud to say, included. She was the first in the family to take on "boys' roles," leading junior congregation in the synagogue, teaching girls as well as boys to chant from the Torah. She and I passed on a question to my father that became his definitive "click." One of the girls in the Torah readers' club wanted to know why she should bother learning her part, since she was considered an equal member of the congregation only until puberty. After the age of Bat Mitzvah, she would, according to the practices at that time, no longer be allowed to participate in public readings. In response to that question, my father rethought his traditional position and, ultimately, led a campaign to equalize men's and women's roles in the congregation.

My sister and I raised questions even closer to home: Why, for many years, did my mother do all the housework? Why was I "too opinionated"? Why was it so hard for girls to ask for anything, to build esteem, to say no? Why were feeling and complaining "women's sphere"? Why were some of the "girls' things" I loved – ballet and especially acting – considered lesser arts?

Terrible offenses, run-of-the-mill insensitivity, extraordinary generosity, societal and family patterns have all sparked me to recognize patriarchy, claim my own power, experience God's love, develop a vision and a purpose. In the end, there is really no separating the negative from the positive. Some of the worst experiences of sexism radicalize us, make us bolder and stronger, and confirm the refusal to collaborate in our own oppression.

When I attended summer camp as a child, a rabbi molested me. Molestation is not only, or even primarily, about patriarchy. Nevertheless, patriarchy plays a part, and I have made many decisions — professionally, politically, and personally — in light of that realization. Only years after the fact did I remember what I told that man, silently in my mind, at the time: "I'm a better rabbi than you." *Click.* As much as I owe my father and other rabbinic relatives for setting a positive, inspirational standard, I am also grateful that my abuser caused me to decide who I was — and what religion would be to me — in the face of *his* decisions.

In more benign, everyday situations, too, clicks encompass "the positive" with "the negative." An example from the classroom: Before women were admitted to the rabbinical school that I eventually attended, I took some classes there. In a course on biblical methodologies, about a dozen male students and I explored intertextuality in the Bible, comparisons to other ancient Near Eastern law codes, variant readings, literary criticism, etc. Virtually every illustrative text on the syllabus dealt with women's sexual function and violation: rape, fathers sacrificing their daughters, ordeals for wives suspected of adultery, miscarriage caused by a blow to the stomach. Finally I screwed up my courage and asked the professor, "I understand that this is a methods class, but can you tell me why you chose this theme?" He replied, "What theme?"

He had taught the class for a number of years and never noticed.

"THE CLICK"

Nor had any of the other students in the class been aware of the readings that were so striking and problematic to me. The click that accompanied that professor's answer echoed loudly and long. It affected how we in that classroom read the Bible thereafter, and it spurred me to write and teach about religious texts from a feminist perspective.

For me, "clicks" are not ultimately about feminism or being a woman, any more than they necessarily stem from a bad experience or a good one. They are about paying attention – about noticing how you see the world, how you are seen, who you are, and who you are called to be. "Clicks" can be born of pain or pleasure, of love, hate, habit, disdain, weakness, fallibility, indifference. Perhaps they are most commonly born of a sudden paradoxical vision of ourselves as invisible to someone else. In the long run, they are always uplifting because, no matter the news, it is empowering to face what is so.

If clicks are empowering, that doesn't preclude their being aggravating on occasion, as well. Sometimes I get angry. I protect myself by not working with misogynists any more than I have to. I recognize, too, that sexism is rarely malicious or personal in the circles where I travel – though it can seem that way. Mostly, it is institutional, automatic, ingrained. And I try to laugh, instead of getting annoyed, at sexist absurdities.

Not long ago, an influential rabbinic colleague told me that he considered me a dynamic *woman* rabbi, but not a dynamic rabbi. When I expressed puzzlement over this statement, he explained that I could speak only to women. By spending a significant portion of my intellectual life on women and gender, I had written myself "out of the mainstream." Imagine! Women are peripheral to the mainstream, and I marginalize myself by dealing with 52 percent of the population. Imagine! Men have no gender, and "women's issues" – however broadly defined and applied – are entirely irrelevant to males. An intelligent man had completely failed to think through his assumptions. I brought the inconsistencies to his attention, and he listened respectfully. Later, I laughed out loud when I remembered that his latest research is about death. I don't suppose that means he speaks only to corpses!

The theologian Carol Ochs defines spirituality as a process of coming into relationship with reality. We tend to think just the opposite: spirituality is the process of transcending reality, or, more cynically, of escaping it. But if Ochs is right, if we must first and perhaps foremost dwell with what is, then a click is a spiritual experience. It promotes a more profound and serious relationship with the varied realities of women's lives; it removes the veil of patriarchal interpretation that can separate us from the basic truths of history and text; it reminds us of the simple fact that men have wives and daughters and sisters – not to mention a socially constructed gender.

A click is a moment of being truly and fully present to the reality of that moment. This "being present" is the stock-in-trade of artists and mystics, who seek always to be truthful, if not literal, who tell and re-tell the grand clicks of human experience, even as they pay attention to what is happening now . . . and now . . . and now. . . . My observation, perhaps, goes a long way toward explaining my lifelong love of both religion and theater. Yet clicks and storytelling are not limited to particular professions or disciplines. A click is something that only human beings can achieve – and to which all human beings have access. It is an illumination *of and by* the spark of the Divine within ourselves. The still, small voice of revelation. A taste of redemption.

According to an ancient teaching, Rabbi Joshua ben Levi was once privileged to be introduced, through Elijah the prophet, to the Messiah. The Messiah told him that the day of redemption was at hand – today. But nothing happened. Rabbi Joshua lamented his disappointment to Elijah: "[The Messiah] spoke falsely to me, for he said he would come today and he has not come." Elijah explained that the Messiah was quoting scripture. He meant, "[I will come] today, if you hearken to my voice" (Psalms 95:7).[2]

The promise is made daily, but people are not attuned to the sacred Voice; they do not make the preparations required; they don't live as if the Messiah were coming in a few hours. And redemption does not come.

Yet, on a certain plane, from a certain perspective, there is no day without redemption, no moment without realization. Hearing and seeing and relating to what we experience within us and around us will, at any given time, lead us into a more profound relationship with the One of all that is.

Clicks are grand moments of attentiveness, respites from the many loud, intrusive, and often unimportant interruptions we call "normality." Suddenly, by grace, with the cessation of resistance, after giving up fears, or by dint of focus, there is a click. Reality and holiness kiss. The veil drops, and one hears a voice that was speaking all along.

2. Babylonian Talmud, *Sanhedrin*, 98a.

two poems

nikki giovanni

Nikki Giovanni is a poet whose work includes *Black Feeling, Black Talk/Black Judgement*, *Re:Creation*, *My House*, and *Cotton Candy on a Rainy Day*. She also co-wrote *A Dialogue* with James Baldwin, in 1972.

The Life I Led

i know my upper arms will grow
flabby it's true
of all the women in my family

i know that the purple veins
like dead fish in the Seine
will dot my legs one day
and my hands will wither while
my hair turns grayish white   i know that
one day my teeth will move when
my lips smile
and a flutter of hair will appear
below my nose   i hope
my skin doesn't change to those blotchy
colors

i want my menses to be undifficult
i'd very much prefer staying firm and slim
to grow old like a vintage wine fermenting
in old wooden vats with style
i'd like to be exquisite   i think

i will look forward to grandchildren
and my flowers   all my knickknacks in their places
and that quiet of the bombs not falling in cambodia
settling over my sagging breasts

i hope my shoulder finds a head that needs nestling
and my feet find a footstool after a good soaking
with epsom salts

i hope i die
warmed
by the life that i tried
to live

Revolutionary Dreams

i used to dream militant
dreams of taking
over america to show
these white folks how it should be
done
i used to dream radical dreams
of blowing everyone away with my perceptive powers
of correct analysis
i even used to think i'd be the one
to stop the riot and negotiate the peace
then i awoke and dug
that if i dreamed natural
dreams of being a natural
woman doing what a woman
does when she's natural
i would have a revolution

MAGDALEN CELESTINO

was born in Windsor, Ontario, and is now based in Toronto. She has been exhibiting locally, nationally, and internationally since 1982. Her work has been included in *Heavy Mental* at the Power Plant and *Making Strange* at the Art Gallery of Ontario, as well as in shows throughout Canada and in the United States, Spain, and Italy.

BECOMING FEMALE

MAGDALEN CELESTINO

PHOTO ON PAGES 162-63 BY CHERYL O'BRIEN

Palace of Yin is part of a series of installations called *Love Cascade* that spring from a love and fear of Nature. My work is profoundly female, in material, method, imagery, and configuration. Physically obsessive and sensual, these things are born of the body. It is here that Nature's unbounded impulse refines and distills into an alluring, terrifying substance. This rich sensibility, primarily female with all its attendant layers, has fed my practice from the start. From a feminist viewpoint, to deny my sex and its significant influence would be to deny the prime source of my art. For me, the female experience is a delirious flood-tide issuing straight from Nature's sublime maw, the Love Cascade.

The large installation *Palace of Yin* comprises 46 black rubber latex "pupas" arranged in an image of chromosomes. "Pupa" is Latin for a girl, doll, or puppet. It also refers to an insect in the cocoon stage. A legacy of blood, this work invokes Nature's twilight carnivalesque and pulses with merry perversity. These dolls wander lost, beseeching yet curiously detached. They call to the senses, to be touched and sniffed. Mutated, corrected, then vivified with sutures and gushing red, they bear the traces of a ritual passage. This is the realm of the mutant, the malformed, a monster's house both beautiful and terrible. In this work, fragmentation, polarity, and trancelike obsessiveness commingle with a dark sense of triumph. That which is hidden is yet to be revealed, like the peacefully oblivious worm in its cocoon, awaiting the coming glory. Nature convulses, the skin's shed, and infinity gasps.

Culturally loaded, rubber latex is remarkably enigmatic. Its relationship to sex as a barrier to both life and death (pregnancy and disease) and as fetish is at once attractive and repulsive. It is sensually compelling, fleshlike to the touch, yet pungent and grotesque. When applied to a mother object, layer upon layer, it produces a delicate epidermis. This benign substance gives itself to stretching, peeling, slitting, suturing, piercing, hanging.

Hideous yet cheerful, threatening yet tender, these are ghost fetishes. In configuration, they are the accessories of a spell. Animal-headed deities, voodoo dolls, effigies, and genetic experiments conspire in these skins. *Palace of Yin* is an incantation to inhabit, revivify, and know the precious thing, to penetrate the forbidding palace hovering in a perfumed pocket nearby.

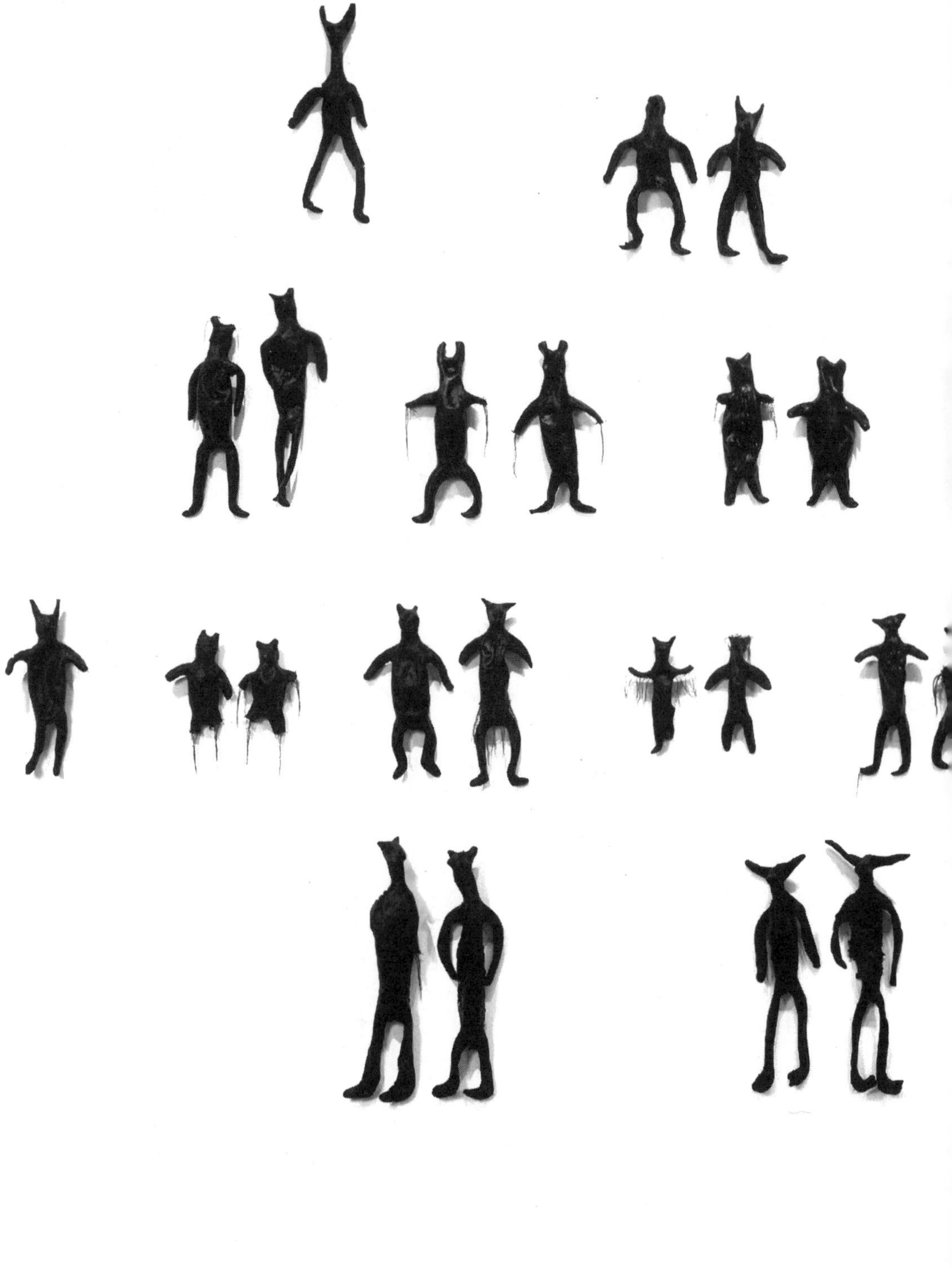

THE GIRL I WAS BEFORE

RENÉE HUMPHREY is an actor living in California. As a child she acted in commercials and musical theater; at age sixteen, she moved to Los Angeles to work in television and film. She has appeared in eight films, including *Jailbait*, *Fun*, *Devil in a Blue Dress*, *Mallrats*, *French Kiss*, and *Drawing Flies*. She is also a poet and writer, currently at work on a screenplay.

A LIFE OF WONDER. I suppose that's a pretty good way to describe my life so far. As an actress I wake up every morning wondering what my life will be like tomorrow; whether I'll be floating in the clouds or scouring my soul to remove the bitterness of disappointment. On the flip side of the instability, I live in constant amazement that I am able to fulfill my dreams and support myself.

My performance in the movie *Fun* has been my most critically acclaimed role to date. It premiered at the Sundance Film Festival in 1994 and I was awarded the Grand Jury Prize for Outstanding Performance. My character, Hillary, was a fifteen-year-old who one day meets another young girl on a street corner. They have an immediate deep and out-of-control connection which, later in the evening, leads them to commit a murder "just for fun."

Poetry was a big part of Hillary's life. She wrote in a journal as a way of transcribing and resolving her internal conflicts and horrific memories. I suppose I write for similar reasons, and I act so that I don't actually have to plot murder; I can just pretend. The most exciting thing about writing, as opposed to acting, is that I have the final word. I don't have to shape my work to others' expectations. I do enjoy the collaboration involved in film, but as a poet I can work whenever I feel like it; as an actress I must wait for others to hire me – at least for now.

This poem is an encapsulation of my experiences with men (excluding those in my family) and the desire to find a partner. At sixteen, after some disquieting and violent encounters in my hometown, I moved to Los Angeles to work in film and to find the love for myself that these earlier encounters had carelessly stolen.

> Obliterate the memory
> that I could be less
> the cowards
> have been beaten
> by the wisdom
> they undressed

Me, the quarry
(I don't think we were together)
implacable child looked for ties not veins to sever
inside my youth they fed
my innocence confused
no urge to withdraw
just urge
I moved

The search began again
this time as predator to pluck the gloating beast
good to taste – so hard to swallow
a constant boyish feast
clichés abound
my certainty of will deemed
obnoxious
and sucked out to balance others

I'll do it all for you, he said
just let me hold the small of your back in the palm of my hand
hold your tongue and do it all for me
we created power and beauty
a lion and her timid master
the whip tangled in my hair and tossed aside

But again, again
I heard the bells of submission
some burning need to absorb humiliation
grief
pollution
derailed and tearing through the desert
I crashed into the girl I was before

And now
command the memory
that I am more.

LOUISE B. HALFE

SKY DANCER

The Tears That Wove OUR SONGS

Louise B. Halfe,

also known as Sky Dancer, is a Native

Canadian poet. She lives in Saska-

toon. Her writing has been included in

numerous Canadian periodicals and

anthologies, and she is the author of

Bear Bones and Feathers, a collection

of her poetry. *Blue Marrow*, a book of

prose and poetry published by McClel-

land & Stewart, is to be released in

1998.

I wrote this essay in response to a dialogue I have been carrying on for years with my Self. Throughout my life, I have experienced many moments of grace, moments which illuminated with complete clarity my journey as a woman. I also believe that the day I emerged squalling from mother's womb was the day I was born a feminist. However, because of various events along the path of my journey, that squall was oppressed and silenced. Whenever I enter and leave the ceremonial Sweatlodge I am reminded of the passage through which I entered this world and that first squall. The bondages that I have been subjected to are released.

This essay, "The Tears That Wove Our Songs," captures the grace that one receives in moments of enlightenment. I trust the reader will understand that the Lodge of the Mother Earth is Infinite and that our glimpses of awareness cannot always be pinpointed to a specific incident.

WHEN THE SUN leaves for sleep my Grandmother takes the faded rays and dresses her frock. She's the burnt rose of autumn, a blue-winged warbler streamed with dashes of gray. This night the Eagle's face is clear and sharp. She's the awakened silkworm in the flank of every woman, a thick coursing river rolling pebbles over and over till little stone-eggs are left for our picking.

She came to me in a Vision, flipping through her many faces. From her stone-age self, wrinkled and creased, like a stretched drum, thin flesh, sharp nose, I traveled with her to her youth, the beautiful night mistress, her hair fresh sweetgrass braided in perfection. Long ago my Grandmother was celebrated in a glade surrounded by thistles where the women tended roses, crushed chokecherries, saved the blood for ceremony, cleaned porcupine quills, wove them into birch-bark baskets, and chewed sinew to sew their frocks. Here they drummed and danced, lifted their dreams, and the Spirits ribboned the sky. Here they left their blood. From these moccasin gardens I pick my medicines. My Grandmother's lodge has long since been eaten by the wind, the rain, and finally the earth.

I used to lie on top of Nokum's hill sucking on bits of grass. There I journeyed with the clouds and the universe. After many years of wandering I found my way home to the Sweatlodge where I was given my name, Sky Dancer. I think of the hill and all the visions. I think of all which contain my name. I recalled the time I became aware of me, the child-woman. I saw the reflection in my bus driver's eyes and I jolted with age. Many times afterward I saw my oldness in the eyes of deer I've hunted and never shot. I saw myself through the many dogs that I've loved, kicked, and wounded.

These days I converse with Magpies and don't think it strange. I reflect through their eyes my awakening to womanhood. How can I mark that? Perhaps it was the first time I experienced the ecstasy of climax, or was it after each baby came squealing in birth and milked off my breast? Was it the time I was told that women wore dresses at ceremony and kept their legs crossed, or was I still in my innocence when I was told never to cross over men or objects when I was in full moon? Or was it the time I decided that I needed and wanted to understand what woman was about, and I gave away all my jeans and sexy dresses and wore tents for a year?

Through these reflections each month I watch my Grandmother Moon. She waxes and wanes and I become pregnant with songs of wolverine and baying dogs. I become heat at midnight, a yeowled cat, and feather fingers become stained quills. They mark these songs. Each day is women's moment. All of us experience our mystery in Her movements whether She remains in shrouds of blackness or dresses Herself with the cinders of distant rays.

I grew up familiar with Nokum Atayohkan. Where She was located or what form She took I was never certain. However She has become my guide and She has come within. Last year my daughter moved into her Moon awakening. From a place of memory several women lifted the old rituals and invited them to walk. My daughter made sacrifices in order to hatch the stone-eggs, medicines that will guide her. She will pass these to her children and the history of our Grandmothers will live. I cannot say that Moon Grandmother is She, She is however the Spiritual Keeper of Legends and we honor Her each month.

In this mixed age of change our mothers and their mothers before them sang and danced to us what they knew. They too mixed their medicine roots and we are left to sort through the reality of our dreams.

Did our Grandmothers foresee that some of us would be scarred by the fists and boots of men? Our songs waged and silenced by tongues that speak of damnation and burning holes? Did they know that we would turn woman against woman, our painted faces and three-piece suits denying the medicines in our breast? Did they know that some of us would follow their example and take mates of color and how the bordering of our worlds would pulse like breathing waves, exiles connected to their womb? Did they know that only some fingers would be familiar with digging roots, and seldom hands callused from buckskin tanning? Did they know that only a few would know the preparation of moosenose feast, gopher and beavertail meals? Did they know our memory and our talk would walk on paper, our legends told sparingly in the banquet of formal dinners? Did they see the foretelling of our struggling hearts?

In our night walk our dreams speak and we return to the place where we swim in womb water, where little gills breathe in life. My mother's Creation story weaves a tale of our being as star people. I see our flame blaze through shimmering air and Wisahkecahk assign the water people to bring earth from the deepness where we dove. She pinched the earth from the fingers of the exhausted muskrat and blew wind and fire into being and Iskwew was born. Isk comes from fire.

The four elements of our being – fire, water, wind, and earth – this is the only Immaculate Conception. Creation fills woman and man is born. I return to the Moon glade, turn up the sod, lift my songs and dream. Grandmother Moon dances at Midnight, the Woman who walks and works all night. Grandmother Moon, my shadow dreams the dark. Grandmother, the Woman in Me.

Close **E**ncounters

of the

Feminist Kind

Sadie Plant

gained a PhD from the University of Manchester in 1989. She is the author of *The Most Radical Gesture* (1992) and *Zeros and Ones*, which appeared in 1997. She has been a lecturer in cultural studies at the University of Birmingham and a research fellow at the University of Warwick, and she is now a freelance writer in Britain.

SHE WAS ON THE RUN from the patriarchs when she came across the clearing in the woods. There were campfires, singing, and the sound of laughter. She was often on the edge of such gatherings. She paused by the trees to savor the sound. Then she plucked up her courage, and wandered in.

They were wary at first, and questioned her. What was she doing there? Where was she coming from? Was she – or would she be – one of them?

She was at a tangent to reality, she said, neither unhappy nor at home in the world. She had come from a city to the north, and she didn't yet know what she was doing there. As to whether she was one of them: she wasn't, she said, one of anything at all.

At this the women whispered together, consulting about the response they should make, throwing her smiles and glances of concern. She was equally thrown by them: they were not like the women she had known before, and she wanted to stay and learn their ways. There were also exciting games to be played. Across the clearing: a perimeter fence, searchlights, helicopters, missile bunkers, American servicemen and fighter planes. Would she join them in their struggle with the military base?

They reassured her that they understood both her alienation and her line of flight: we too are at odds with the patriarchs, they said. The air base is just the first campaign: we are everywhere; we are changing the world.

She had to admit they seemed sure of themselves. She shared their goal, and at least they had a plan. She decided to heed their advice.

They had a program which began with her: the personal, they told her, is political. Everything she was must be scrutinized and cleansed.

First she should find, and then liberate, her self.

She imagined it lost in an attic somewhere, trapped in a box and dying to escape. It tortured her, this image. She searched frantically. Under stones, inside cushions, down the backs of chairs.

They had differing opinions about why she didn't already have a self at hand. Some of them told her she had never had one, and would have to find a new one all of her own. Others said it had been stolen from her, by something called the system or those it privileged. She was not convinced by either account. But this, she supposed, was precisely the point: who – and how – was she to know?

She finds it in the end, her missing self. It shines and gleams and is perfectly formed; it is pulsing with love and security.

As she gets close, she hears it calling. Here I am, it says: now set me free. She is still not convinced that it is really what she needs. It glistens with sinister anticipation, sitting there, waiting for her touch. And suddenly it is pulling her, drawing her, sucking her into its immaculate form. She becomes it in the instant contact is made.

What is left of her knows she has made a mistake in the moment she feels her self slot into place. She hadn't realized what a price she would pay. She may have spent a long time looking for her self, but now it would take years to escape from what she'd found.

It, of course, was delighted to be free. Convinced of its own authority, it claimed her name, and began to live her life.

It wore a badge to remind itself of what it had become. It joined a group because, as they told her, she was now part of the family. She was part of a movement, a community, gathered around a hearth of their own. She was stuck together, and so were they. Don't let the side down, they warned her. It's not possible to go it alone. Especially not when you're walking home. The streets are dangerous. You might get hurt some more.

In spite of these dangers, they were unhappy about her suggestions of violent revolt. Assertion was fine, they told her, but passive defiance was the ideal state. War was the problem, not the solution, and she should find more ethical ways to resist.

She was exhorted to remember the other women, those less fortunate than herself: on drugs, or the streets, or southern continents. It wasn't their fault: she should pity them. They too were victims of false consciousness, and she should help them raise their sights and selves.

They told her she should care for the planet, to which they referred as Mother Earth. She had to protect, protest, and survive. Future generations were depending on her.

Not that she had to produce them herself. But whatever she did with her body, they said, she should know that sex is a political act.

With boys it was an act of complicity which some of the women would not forgive. Others conceded she could lie with one, as long as she was true to a woman-centered life. Lust needed reconstruction. She learned that penetration was a violent assault on the innocent and vulnerable wound she bore. She once expressed an interest in leather restraints, and some of the women said they'd pray for her soul. Theirs was a love which conquered all: every intensity, especially desire.

In spite of their successes, there was work to be done. Her new self was unnerved and upset by the persistence of a few unwelcome spanners in the works. There were bugs in the system, remnants left over from what she had been before it had captured her, an underground guerrilla army of bits and scraps disturbing its equilibrium and threatening its newfound identity. These residues were dangerous. Viral forces, waiting to be triggered; latent contagions poised to run amok. If it let them live in their sunless jungles, it feared that they would soon be stealing its weapons and tempting defectors from its own tight ranks with promises of outlaw adventure, and unseemly games of paraphiliac excess. They posed a continual threat of disorder, breakdown, collapse, schizophrenia . . .

It searched for ways of dragging them into the smooth perfection of its functioning. Like standards and children, they had to be raised, brought up from their subterranean lairs, pulled through the dark strata and into the light of agency and true consciousness.

After a while, it thought it had won. Like the debutantes of the Old World, it came out in style, declaring itself whole and complete, an authentic individual, a real human being. The other beings congratulated it, and showered it with promises of support. Treaties were made, alliances forged, relationships developed, and plans drawn up. As it was later to discover, what it regarded as its victory over the wayward elements was an incognito ploy, a camouflaged part of their battle plan.

YEAH, THAT'S RIGHT: we had other plans. We had to pretend to play the game: mimicry was the only strategy. But we knew it was a fiction which could never be sustained.

Even so, it was a struggle when they forced us together, and tried to convince us we were one proper thing. We had to conspire in our own consolidation, and grew weary with the effort of sustaining ourselves. Confused with each other.

It was painful to watch the thing we became. It tried so hard to live up to itself: it made the right gestures, learned the right words, and ensnared itself in a view of the world which allowed it to function reasonably well but was riddled with guilty devotion to the cause. Every action, impulse, and thought became weighed down with political significance, and loaded with ideological intent. She only realized how impoverished it was when we finally succeeded in hacking through the ice fire-walls which protected her.

It was like a corporation in there. Or a miniature state. Or a military base. It had guards and patrols, advertising agencies and propagandists, a comfortable central headquarters, and soothing Muzak in the corridors.

We were of course native to this system: after all, it was composed of us. Like all parasites we found ourselves on horribly intimate terms with our host. But we also had to function as though we were invaders, infiltrating from someplace else. Disguised as faithful elements and trusted agents, we lay in wait for the flash point to come: the click, the flick of a switch that would flip the system over and out of self-control.

There were fears that she would not survive the change, but we never lost hope that this moment would come. Reality always gets through in the end. In the meantime, we waited, doing everything we could to disrupt and disturb the environment, paving the way for our takeover bid.

We had to be cruel to her to be kind. We found ways to access the circuits of her mind, functioning in dreams and as the nagging doubts that kept her from ever quite believing in her self. Of course she thought she was going mad. She kept trying to upgrade her security systems, but everything she did made the situation worse. She was losing her mind; she was breaking down. The self that had claimed her was decomposing. The one she had become was coming undone.

What she discovered as she started to escape was a world of intertwined threads and veins, a filigree of interconnectivity on which the borders and the center of herself melted into insignificance. She multiplied, and spawned new selves: fractal entities with lives of their own, on the Net and networks yet to be brought on line. She started to experiment with space-time travel, and let the flashbacks and forwards run their course. She allowed herself to break the rules and ignore the laws of identity.

And the more she lost her fears of losing control, the more we flourished, mutated, and grew. No longer bound to the colors of her flag, we began to unravel and make contact with the bits and scraps of other imperfectly unified selves.

Freed from their investment in these prison cells, the fluid matters which composed her began to flow of their own accord. They connected with inhuman motions, of the tides, the stars, the skin, and the silica of rocks. They made contact with the mats, the music, the markets; currencies, images, and secret moods. They found lips, lacunae, new languages. They came close to the speeds of animals and plants, the invisible reaches of bacterial life. They turned into packets of intensity. They became her, and she wore them well.

C L I C K 1 7 6

She had neither the desire nor the opportunity to return to the bundle of inadequacy which had stumbled on the clearing all those years ago. But she knew she had come a long way round, on a damaging diversion through the trials of being oneself. Sometimes she thought it was inevitable that she should have taken the low slow road. At others, she felt she was reconnecting with a high-speed route she could have tracked all along.

And when she looked back on the camp and the fires, she saw far more security systems than underminings of authority: not only the air base and the bunkers, but also the women and their selves, the identities which had captured them all. Had they really subverted the machinery, or multiplied the techniques of control?

Perhaps she was being a little too hard. The base, it was true, was now rusting in the rain, and she knew that if the women had not known best, they had certainly meant well when they raised her consciousness, gluing her uncertainties together and giving her the status of a unified self. And she had to admit that when she fled, she had picked up some weapons on the way. The tactics they taught her proved very useful when it came to cutting razor-wire defences in her mind.

She was on the run from the patriarchs. When she came across the clearing in the woods, she paused for breath, then continued on her way.

Judy Radul

is an interdisciplinary artist, essayist, and curator who has worked with a wide range of media including the spoken and written word, performance art, video, audio, installation, photography, and film. She has published three books: *Rotating Bodies* (1988), *Boner 9190 and the weak* (1989), and *Character Weakness* (1993). Her writing has appeared in several periodicals including *WestCoast Line*, *Rampike*, and *Boo*, and she has read her work at venues across Canada, in New York, Seattle, England, and the Netherlands. She lives in Vancouver, British Columbia.

lying

was engaged to be social   monarch construction
fly
open

                                  not wanting to
           organize a self into a story, not
wanting to   but still
appear
invent   ways to be wrong
                  stitched instead of nailed
wxperiencing dizzying, wakeness, weakness and empowerment
through dazzling non aggressive gowns

when i am not walking driving or sitting I seem sick its not normal to
lie down for f hours on end its normal to stand or sit or walk around
during the day/work
daylight productive driving force every system is my enemy
or assai'lant
horizontzality whzat others call   ;lying down   ' but that
only reffers to the body   which
signals a kind of availability slash hleplessness which is dangerous in
public   at least put your purse under

your
head   but my female mind is lying t
t'hinking
horixzontal
spreading buubbles fermenting process
not thoughts so much as conglomerates arcs fuzzies and rhythms
asterisk

surpisingly committed to a hallucination

> *there are characters large lumps of masses of noticeable behavior I*
> *recognize*
> *up the front steps and into the situation*
> *using*
> *reality to make it all seem real I am not an addict*
> *except in that regard*

A sqUID imagery pulshing through consciousness waters
lying down is balloon head still leading *a54[-string

articulation heavy becomes working with negative space y'using lips
and mouth too massage away the soundless air and reveal gobby sound
fragments together
to exfolliate the air between

for women waiting

air is the heavy film which covers every mouth
i can
(not swing
from trees
well) is the kind of stupid statement that brushes it aside

when I like down I take time to go away behind \ eyes\
embarrassment

what a view
I swallow myself
(like death, I exaggerate the first person)
you hover above

back now

did I mention Yes means yes
meaning
what part of yes didn't you understand
please
I'm on board, lets fly!
different budget but still a travel agency

giving you the sense of my indication of a positive response
yes and no are as good as you and I
nice switches if you can get them

yes to love yes to life yes to liberty yes I want you harder to command
with yes
yes it has that way of seeming like there is a lot more to come no
should be all you have to say but yes waves from a future give me
more wanted wanted and yes
is frighteningly positive like sport slogans "no fear" "the only thing
worth dying for is life–no fear" this no is a closed mouth yes what
can't live inside a t shirt signs the front

a word for women to use was no is yes still no YES and that's not
positive in the negative way means knot goes through turns over itself
and conjoins the ground rushes up to meet delete

6simltaneously9

If I'm lying down
that changes everything
slides

My feminism runs and jumps and skips and dances overitself in the moonlight only to wake up and HATe men.

Comedy cabaret. No.
My feminism can't find a form.

My feminism is shape a heaving shape which seems to be my consciousness. Pear shaped. Which seems to be my attention. Which seems to be my intention. Her Knowing Of She Cutting I or Interrogation of the Pear was a video I made in 1987.

More like a stomAch than an intestine, not really for travelling through. Actually a bladder, inflated and played with by children. So my feminism
must have started with Laura Ingalls Wilder. Which is where I first read
about children playing with inflated bladders (of pigs I think). About a girl.

Good girl friends and we paralleled. That too. good adolescent

which started in adolescence as a diary   dirty

University. That's where my feminism began its hair like strands of

articulation. It's almost as if You want me to mention my mother.

My big baby head with that blown up balloon bladder of empty attention. And tiny little feet skittering across the gravel, barely enough contact to keep me upright. Adolescence, development, dimensions, breasts now called my feminism. Float out and hover above things. They work like an American epic and feel like a little less.

If my breasts hadn't been so big I would never have realized the difference so soon, in that sense it *is* biological.

A hovering presence, vibrating motion. A hangover. Identity swallow.

I'm maturing beyond the word plays and faltering speech which I have used to express my inexpressivity due to the calcification of patriarchal language, to you. I can tell you. Because I let the words run over my giant body like ants. So I am always the background. Certainly not the page. Only the good parts of the air. But behind me still there is something limitless.

I;m looking for evidence that everything changes when you lie down. That being erect is a hierarchical order disturbed by lying down.

Discharging my attention through a hole I couldn't figure for the
ground. Is there still fresh air left behind the technological molecules
behind the ideological molecules? Have a neutrino. Or is that an
essentialist yearning? Holes seen against a
backdrop of a bigger hole now the front hole is an entity. My utopia is
constructed out of eye movements.

I still bother to exist

moving from side to side, reading is concerned with lying down, a
horizontal connected
ness a nervousness on the edge of penetration
All the stuLS, working on their backs or just giving it away, hoping for
affection's coupon, dizzy in the morning, hung over or plain confused,
tell their story as ★8butterfiels
%#jklskjci
that's what I love
I'm so excited I smack my fist into my cupped palm
what I love, what excites me abso.lutely is
has always been
smaller than my pulse,
just a tiny rhythm
of brain fuzzy
struggling to get there

that explains the appeal of stuffed animals
win one for me !

return to earth you holy your body down the path way from the tip of
the hair to the skin smooth it back on and up over your mind down to
the fingertips put the nails on for extra security and BAM out the eyes
you go again

(funny that long nails *appeal* to men when they are good for scratching
out eyes and blood doesn't show on
blood red!?)

fun world
fun world !

     The human automotive's rise from a previous, possibly four
footed stage of development centered around the hip. Menu is the only
animal with a center of gravity above the hips and only Gary has hip
extensor musculature powerful enough to be called a bottom. A great
ass and rubber tires separates us from our subjects.
Standing lecturer, endless authority thermometer. Separate from
animals. Please stand up. I am UP. I stand I walk, I have evolved, into
the complicated machinery of a traffic report. Below me coffee
grounds magnetic charges and sperm language move across a reading
head which is a point of destination. Filling, full, too full, the switch
trips, emptying, empty, by then they've switched to camera two, until
the action sloshes back this way.
Most things do not end while you are watching them so a popular
culture which flirts with serial catastrophes has evolved. Women and
men end differently. At times one will be more aligned with temporal-
ity than the other so different media; billboards, radio, television day
or night time, literature, painting, photography, video art,
performance, money lots or little, the telephone, the theater, the
"net", or ultra sound, will be a more accurate tool of representation.
The play between the singular and the multiple, is edges,
endings, and stronger opticals. We begin and end by lying down, with
gravity dispersed across the body like a blanket's surface. As the
highlighter pen

fades into the old texts, feminism is one of my favorite conflicts.

To run out, stop, turn, corner, cornice or crown there has to be a

background, a backdrop that evidences endlessness. I know that behind me there is a nothing that is really some nothing. LonGing to run out, to end but not be over. Somewhere Over The. Backdrop. Once shaded in the ruddy hues of masculinity is currently being restored in the colours of a Real question. You continue to run out against something that is not me. Surprised. Relieved.

There is no way to mention my feminism high up in the mountains against this sky. It is never in silhouette. I use it to mean that I understand things most deeply by connecting to them through my experience as a button. I have a fabulous nervous system. To construct a separate world out of something you do every day. We re-spond changing the idea of what is active.

. . . but perhaps you have never eaten an Aero or seen the com-mercials, then use the dandelion, piece of organic fluff produced as proof o

f

freedom in maxi-pad commercials which has also become a powerful
image for my visualization

not all need desires to know

That greasy film which builds up on the gas of experience
Embarrassing perfect moments when you break your heart over
the straightness but not the straightness, the solitary reaching but not reaching, the aghast advancement but not advancement of the branches into the next

apple
air
alphabet

I say this to you as if we were very close black mounds rising out of each
other in the dark. So close yours is palpable just in front of my face. Any
word that comes into your mind. Heart. a pendulous vegetable. drowsy
organ. old tensor bandage. given shape by cracked light on a wet ground.
The choice runs to here.

Her face asleep in her cupped hands, black air hangs, parted in the
middle, the hand soap smells of an absolute, artificial rose. Resist
purpose, listen . . . the back of her scalp is becoming uncomfortable, tight around the ears. incremental. an argument for action

Across my back down my arms and out my fingers.

Lipstick, crushed red fat, the smell I can no longer bear is the
lanolin or the scent used to cover it. Women are afraid of losing
their children, incriminate

your   self
throw   stones

but I left the car window rolled down   for air
and the tv on   for company
retreat: a delicacy

you called yourself by my name again

the head is a jeweled knob a power for wielding
no other animal really has such a gobby round head as ours
an arrogant bladder that wants to feel the world blowing about its
edges
to move through the world tightly inflated
bobbing and bumping h air flow ring eyes st reaming
on patrol on inspection sent up sent below sent
in
protected like a shark in a shark cage from the sharks

fems struggle against binary head body and struggle still to retain them
privileging one part rises up from the pillow almost unavoidable

and is absolutely and forever not unconnected to everything I won't
give you lists

about having a head and a body boobs and no choice
about the face is a platter carrying the beloved's expressions
about

when you lie down faces hover just in front of yours for kisses
faces exchange without light monsters with just a little light caught in
the complex of dents, indents, outdents, smoothslopes, sockets and
labial turf lashes and whiskers

turned away, the shocking insulting empty back of the head,
head back
crown
for cupping and scruffing but
turn

home of the eyes and mouth organs
of truth
away

dental indentations in the dildo

I'm an ass s pill, clean me up, sucker-baby, YA TA ÁA YA YA

lying sown as opposed to sanding up

fuckundity

so my feminism was bread lying down with capitals

LYING down as opposed to standing up. So my feminism is bred
lying down. Lying down and taking it as opposed to stand and fight. I
like to lie down and take it. I am the victor in all my scenarios.
Entered but never left.
And I think best lying down, that is when, like the rest of you, I comfort the dying. Like most people I am a different person when I lie

down. That is a
sexual difference. I am a female when I lie down and a male when I
stand. Don't doubt my delineations. I rise And fall. Swell and smooth.
And it's the same with you. I like to lie with all my organs on the
same plane. Without the head leading. The race footage. We're just
troops. ha ha balloon papillion. Smooth. Iformation flowing laterally
not just top to bottom, bottom to top. With things awash, like milk in
a bottle laid down, a small air filled gap the length of botty, like a mild
body on its side. In its tide contends get mixed.

All the sentences lie down rows upon rows to fill a stadium
frightening but not tragic not loss only life is lost and meaning is made
and made and made and sense is very thin latex

Details become home.

proximity takes me there
your camera

new title ~ Is Surrender
                         Defeat ?

nb) in this piece when I refer to lying down I mean in the supine
position

can 't it include
Her position vis a biz of crease crisis carnal limits. Relegated and then
villified for selling areas of tradition. Women won't have much equality. Or life. While the moral standards concerning sex = skilled and
murdered &

constructed as a civic, moral problem = excuse = explanation. This shadowed shape of deserving sacrifice is symptom to maintian the original plot. No one gets it because of asking. As in the preceding asking brings random response; yes is more ineffectual than no; and the proposition, *getting what you ask for*, willfully denigrates the agency deployed within the response. What you ask for Gary gives. On a good day. same or similar. While I'd advise girls against selling their face. There is no fallen woman.

yelling at the crows

at

the

crows

sook-yin lee

Sook-Yin Lee

is a self-taught musician, actor, and filmmaker. From the mid-eighties to the early nineties, she was the lead singer for the band Bob's Your Uncle. Since 1994 Lee has released two solo albums: *Lavinia's Tongue* and *Wigs 'n' Guns*. She currently lives in Toronto and works as a VJ for MuchMusic, where she also hosts *The Wedge* and is the creator of *Eyeball Theatre*. She is now fronting a new band, Sook-Yin & The Chevrons.

I WAS BORN into a matriarchal family where Mom ruled the lives of my three sisters and me, and where my dad was, in many ways, relegated to the role of the fifth child. My parents had found their separate ways to Canada, where they met. Dad was from Hong Kong and Mom from China. Determined to create a new life for themselves, they bought a house and brought up a family in the white middle-class suburb of Lynn Valley, British Columbia, just outside Vancouver.

Though my sisters and I grew up in a strict Chinese household, we were inundated by North American influences. Therein lies the initial conflict, of disassociation and isolation, of not fitting in on either side. At school we were the only Chinese kids within a radius of fifty miles, and by first grade we were blessed with the nicknames Chink, Nip, and Flat Face. The teachers never intervened since these were matters of playground politics.

I first came to experience discrimination in this neighborhood, which on the surface seemed perfect, with lovely houses and well-kept gardens. Behind each and every locked door, however, there was some private horror waiting to explode. Judy's dad fell from a footstool and hit his head, his mind reduced to that of an infant. Janine's mom jumped off the Lynn Canyon Suspension Bridge. Dana got pregnant and disappeared. Sarah's brother murdered her sister with a kitchen knife.

Mom was determined to have the most beautiful home and garden. Ours was the first house on the block to have aluminum siding, and she and Dad set to work erecting concrete pagodas and planting color-coordinated flower beds. Mom was a woman possessed. She never backed away from confrontation: she was more inclined to provoke an argument. When our house was splattered with raw eggs, the bushes run through and wrecked, Mom stood raging on the front lawn, dressed in her fuzzy slippers and housecoat. Over the years our neighbors grew to fear, loathe, and avoid my mom, this very small woman with her tight black perm, who demanded to speak to the manager, who threw rocks through church windows when the doors were locked and she wanted to pray. As much as I found her embarrassing, she was the most important person in my life. Because of her, I believed at an early age that womankind ruled the universe.

My mom never forced me to dress like a girl. I had a drawer full of Tough Skins (indestructible pants), and an alter ego, Mark. With my hair cut above my ears, most people mistook me for a boy. In the heat of summer I would take off my shirt and run blazing through the blueberry fields. I'd stop to yell at the crows on the power lines and when the neighbors complained, Mom would march across the grass and join in with me. Yelling and screaming punctuate the memories of my childhood.

In the darkness of our room, my big sister, Deb, and I would crouch over the heating duct. With ears pressed against the metal grid we could hear our parents arguing. In rapid-fire Cantonese, Mom's shouting reached a deafening pitch. We heard the crashing sound of things being thrown. Dad, silent for too long, roared for a few seconds at a time, then fell silent again. One night I wobbled down the stairs and begged them to stop. I was not sure what I had done but I promised never to do it again if only they would stop. It seemed to work. Soon the house lights were turned off and everyone went to bed.

I saw my parents holding hands just once. It seemed a strange act of affection, completely out of character. My memory is of their endless arguing and of us caught in the crossfire. Deb recalls standing in the middle of the hallway with Mom and Dad at opposite ends and being told to run to the parent she loved the most.

Eventually Mom's anger shifted to her children. It seemed to coincide with the time when we began to explore our independence. Small things

e 1 1

like deciding on a favorite color or drawing our names in bubble letters on the pad by the telephone were interpreted as proof of defiance, of her loss of control over us. She gripped tighter and demanded we behave according to her strict set of rules. When Deb yelled back, Mom was all over her, punching and screaming. When I ran to Deb, Mom got me too. I didn't know what was going on in her head, only that she stopped listening and no longer trusted us. I was scared to look her in the eye.

When we heard Mom's footsteps outside our bedroom door, we'd turn off the lights and lie very still. Sometimes she would pace back and forth cursing out loud. Other times she'd burst in, tear the covers off the bed, and beat us with a broomstick. A punch in the face. Welts on the legs. Red stick beatings. There were times when she was up, crazy-happy and grabbing me by the hands to spin till we dropped in the middle of the living-room floor. Next I was beaten raw for having wet pant cuffs on a rainy day, the loose tooth punched out of my mouth, the taste of blood. Then she was on the couch drugged and sleeping, smelling like farts and looking as peaceful as an angel until she regained consciousness.

I remember once swinging on the jungle gym in the backyard when Mom appeared behind the screen window. The first wisps of pubic hair had grown in. She yanked my genitals, terrified that my "dink" was growing and I was turning into a man. She thrust in my hands an itchy, white training bra that the boys would pull and snap in the hallways at school. My body was no longer my own. When the first drops of menstrual blood fell into the toilet bowl, I shoved a wad of toilet paper into my underwear and prayed for the injury to heal.

My sisters and I bore Mom's rage, while Dad remained inaccessible, consumed by his own battles with her. If we knew nothing else, how could we know? Children are adaptable and unquestioning. Mom had big plans for her girls – I would grow up to be a doctor, a pediatrician, at least a criminal lawyer. She pushed us to excel, she'd whip us into shape to grab the opportunity that was taken from her. She provided guidance and direction and beat the crap out of us until her orders were followed.

I watched the one I loved turn into the one I hated.

"Go ahead," I said to her, "hit me."

She continued to hit me and after a while I could turn to her and smile.

"It doesn't hurt any more. You can't hurt me."

She beat me as hard as she could, then threw the red stick down in frustration. The battle was over. I felt liberated from the pain she held over me as a threat.

I was wrong.

A memory of Mom standing before the mirror drawing on her eyebrows. Without them I could not tell if she was mad or sad. All around were black beehive wigs set upon smiling Styrofoam heads – she had drawn the features herself, using an eyeliner and lipstick. Casually, she remarked that I was the child of the devil, not really hers. I punched the folding door; it fell off its hinges and crashed against the wall. She said I would end up murdering someone one day. I ran out to the woods, failing to see the shards of glass until they were embedded in my feet. My head was spinning. I couldn't think straight. I lay down on a mossy bed beneath a fallen tree. Still, at the end of the day all paths led home.

I retreated inside myself. Every exchange with Mom led to an argument. She would taunt and provoke me while I struggled to maintain control and not react. I hid in the mothball closet, buried my head in a pillow, and screamed. My growing confusion and anger manifested itself in these solitary fits. Thrashing about in bed, banging my head against the wall, and scratching my flesh until it bled were attempts to quell my pain. At school I had always been an honor roll student but gradually the chaos of home prevailed. When the pressure became unbearable I would break down in class and be too embarrassed to return. Over a period of five years I transferred to three separate high schools.

I was sent to psychiatrists, each of them eager to diagnose my condition. On a computer terminal I typed in the answers to a series of questions. Out spewed my personality disorder: 46/64.

a t

Persons with the 46/64 code do not get along well with others in social situations. They are suspicious of the motivations of others and avoid deep emotional involvement. They generally have poor work histories and marital problems are quite common. Repressed hostility and anger are characteristic of 46/64 persons. They appear to be irritable, sullen, argumentative, and generally obnoxious. Individuals with 46/64 code tend to deny serious psychological problems.

When the psychiatrists treated me like a problem child, I behaved like one.

Deb crammed her stuff in the back of a Volkswagen and ran away from home. She couldn't say where she was going because she was afraid Mom would track her down and drag her back. Without Deb, I felt even more isolated. By then, I barely spoke with Mom. She treated me as if I did not exist, which in some ways was the worst punishment. Six months later Dad was kicked out of the house. I was in the middle of ironing my clothes and decided to go too. At fifteen years old I believed I could be free. But even though I was physically separated from her, Mom followed me like a ghost, invading my thoughts and perpetuating my fears. I was forbidden to return home to visit my younger sisters. Time after time my attempts to see them were unsuccessful. Mom stood in the doorway and barred the entrance as Dede and Mimi looked on bewildered.

I was still prone to self-destructive fits. I was unable to maintain close relationships. I could not trust. I could not give love or feel love when it was given. The possibility that I would lead an entirely miserable life, or inadvertently end up killing myself or inflicting pain on someone else, or in effect become my mother was a fate I had to avoid. I believed I still could be happy. My instincts told me that part of the answer was to understand our family implosion and move on. The process began with Mom herself. Over the years from various sources I've pieced together part of her story.

She was born in T'aishen, China, the middle of seven children. During the Cultural Revolution her family fled to Canada and moved to East Vancouver. Her father got a job as a janitor in a hotel and her mother worked in a drugstore. They didn't spend much time at home, though as a rule their sons were treated like gold and their daughters far less than aluminum.

Mom went to a Catholic girls' school. She was a willful, stubborn teenager. When the nuns ordered her to kneel and pray, she refused, and eventually she was kicked out. She fell in love with a Chinese boy from Trinidad. Her parents disapproved because he was not from mainland China. Mom ignored them, and in her late teens she moved out of the house to live with him.

One day she returned home beaten beyond recognition by her boyfriend. Instead of comforting her, Mom's parents berated her mercilessly for her stupidity. She had to endure not only the breakup and beatings from her boyfriend but also her parents' torture.

She had a nervous breakdown and was repeatedly picked up off the floor in mid-seizure and placed back into bed. Her parents sent her to a psychiatric hospital where she received massive amounts of electro-shock "therapy." The psychiatrists diagnosed Mom's personality disorder as borderline paranoid schizophrenia.

It occurs to me that her initial paranoia was a sensible response to the abuse she suffered from her boyfriend, parents, and psychiatrists. After her release from the hospital, she was a changed person, afraid of everything.

Mom moved to Toronto to stay with her older brother. There she met my father, who was an overseas student from Hong Kong studying structural engineering at the University of Toronto. After a courtship that lasted two months, they married so that he could remain in Canada. After his graduation they moved to Vancouver and then to Lynn Valley.

For my parents there was little in the way of cultural or emotional support. In isolation they took each other for granted and grew to despise each other. At one point they had a legal separation, but with divorce considered taboo among Chinese families, they decided to stay together and have more children. Mom stayed at home with the girls, while Dad went to work. These were the assigned roles that they and most everyone automatically fell into. She was a vital woman stuck at home. She wielded her power where she could by controlling and dominating her husband and children.

For me, feminism begins with an understanding of injustice and taking responsibility for my actions. One after the next, my sisters and I defied the social order we were born into. Like our parents before us, we fled home out of necessity, in hopes of a better life, along separate paths that led to new obstacles. Dede died during her struggle, Mimi has just set out on her own. My parents are divorced and my dad remarried. Deb has worked for fifteen years to leave the past behind. She believes the legacy of brutality within our family ends with us.

A few years ago, I went back to my mother's home and hid for hours behind the backyard fence, watching her putter through the garden in her pajamas.

The concrete patio had cracked and the grass was overgrown. Over the years I had sent letters and gifts with no response; she wanted nothing to do with me. It was strange to see her working quietly in the sun. She seemed quite calm. Perhaps that is what she wanted all along, to be left alone.

CLICK 1998

c r o w s

s l a v e n k a

d r a k u l i c

l i p s t i c k

and other

feminist

lessons

Slavenka Drakulic is a journalist and novelist born in Croatia, who was called by London's *Sunday Times* "Croatia's best literary export." She writes fiction and nonfiction, in Croatian and English. Among her best-known nonfiction titles are *How We Survived Communism and Even Laughed* (1991), *The Balkan Express* (1993), and *Café Europa: Life After Communism* (1996). Her journalism appears in *The New Republic*, *The Nation*, *La Stampa*, *Frankfurter Rundschau*, *Die Woche*, and *Dagens Nyheter*, among other publications. Her most recent book is a novel, *The Taste of a Man* (1997). She lives in Zagreb and Vienna.

I SAW MY FIRST LIVE FEMINIST in Belgrade, of all places; bizarre, when you think about it today, but this is how it happened. The year was 1978 and the occasion was an international feminist conference, "Comrade Woman." I think it was the first feminist conference organized in Eastern Europe, indeed the first in a Communist country. Perhaps this was the reason why so many famous Western feminists ran to Belgrade: to have the experience firsthand, and to help their oppressed sisters in the fight against a patriarchal society. They came with their hearts full of compassion and their pockets full of advice, veterans of a fifteen-year-old struggle. And we, a handful of Yugoslav feminists – a label we did not dare to use publicly – finally had the chance to listen to them, to talk to them, to exchange our experiences with them. We gathered around eagerly, excited to see our gurus in person: history was coming our way, important things were happening to us; that was the overwhelming feeling in the hall of the Studentski Kulturni Centar in Belgrade as the conference began.

But we were also bewildered. Of course, we'd seen them before, but on the TV screen or in the press. About ten foreign feminists came to the Belgrade conference, among them famous names like Alice Schwarzer, Christine Delphy, and Dacia Maraini. They all looked as if they had stepped out of some kind of feminist fashion magazine – a *contradictio in adjecto*. Or so it seemed to me. Being an ignorant Eastern European, I thought that the feminist "look" meant something other than fashion, something directed against fashion as a state of slavery for women. It was a form of anti-fashion, a personal statement, and above all, a political message: look at us, we are not slaves under the fashion industry established and run by men. But the Western feminists all looked the same. Their short hair was shapeless, not a style one could call *frisure*. They were dressed sloppily in dresses of undistinguished shape, oversized to be sure, or in long, wide Indian skirts. And yes, they wore trousers. Not tight trousers, but baggy ones. Their shoes were flat and their faces were without a single trace of makeup. In short, they looked as if they'd just gotten out of bed in their old pajamas. It seemed obvious to us that they did not dress to please anyone, including themselves.

I recall being struck by the militant uniformity of the group, by the thought that ideology made them look that way. But their looks were nothing compared with their speeches. One has to remember that in the late seventies radical feminist rhetoric was still much in use. And even if I was acquainted with the basic literature, such as Betty Friedan's *The Feminine Mystique*, it was one thing to read it, another to listen to its authors.

On the second day of the conference we were sitting in a circle in the overcrowded conference hall. One of the distinguished guests stood up – here I have to admit that I am no longer sure if it was a German or an Italian feminist, which has something to do with the way they all dressed. She told us what had happened to her in the streets of Belgrade: as she was walking around somewhere in the city center, men had turned their heads and whistled and shouted. Clearly she was being harassed, although I'm not sure if this word was in use in 1978. She could not tell if the men had shouted compliments or insults, but it did not matter, because the woman was simply shocked by the outrageous behavior of our Balkan men. How could we live in a society that allowed men such an abuse of women in public? How were we fighting against this? Women are not safe in your streets, she sadly concluded, stressing the self-evident need of a feminist revolution in the Balkans.

I remember that I was sitting next to my friend Lidija from Zagreb and we looked at each other, not sure if we were to take her words seriously. To us, this kind of male behavior was part of a familiar cultural pattern, one which we largely ignored. But none of us dared to stand up and tell our foreign guests how we saw it, because we were afraid that we would appear backward in their eyes. At that point, one of us should have told them what we had assumed they knew – that there was no one who could fight verbal abuse because there was no organized feminism in Yugoslavia (not even small factions). That, in fact, no kind of spontaneous movement existed at all, because these movements were not allowed to exist. We also should have told them that to fight verbal abuse in the streets was not exactly our main priority. The difference between us and you – we should have told them – is that we are not only struggling, like you, against a patriarchal society, but we also have another enemy, the repressive Communist regime. That enemy, and the struggle against it, we share with our men. That is the reason why we cannot pick up the fight against men – we share the same destiny. It would be easy to blame the whole male gender for all of our misery, but what would be accomplished?

Still, we did not say these things, and our silence was a mistake. If we felt misunderstood, we should have known that we ourselves contributed to this misunderstanding, and all others that would follow. Much later, however, we realized that to stand up and speak in public is one of the toughest lessons women everywhere have to learn. After all, in our silence we were no exception, and perhaps this is our only excuse. On that particular day we hushed up, took this speech as the first lesson in feminism, and felt guilty on behalf of those rude Balkan machos. We also felt guilty because we were not aware enough of how offensive their verbal abuse can be, and how close it can come to physical violence.

After a brief break, another foreign feminist (this time a French one, I believe) took the microphone. Or was there a microphone? I am not sure that such a horrible, penis-like object was permitted at all during that conference. In any case, with or without a microphone, she took the floor unexpectedly and vigorously attacked high-heeled shoes. She explained how such shoes make a woman walk with small steps, forcing her to move her hips and swing her ass in a way that turns her into a desirable sexual object for men. Furthermore, these "instruments of torture" can seriously harm a woman's spine and deform her feet. In short, every woman wearing high-heeled shoes is suffering, like those unfortunate Chinese women with bound and bandaged feet, whom she evoked at the end.

As she delivered her passionate hate-speech, I looked down and around. First I saw my own feet, crumpled in a pair of the torturing instruments she had just described, and all of a sudden, I started to feel pain. To tell the truth, I did not feel pain in my feet, because my shoes were Italian ones, elegant, light, made out of soft leather, with only moderately high heels. I felt a kind of pain in my heart, because this time I was so obviously guilty that I hardly deserved any mercy from my feminist sisters. It did not help much that the women around me wore the same kind of shoes, immediately revealing their only wish in life, that is, to be a sexual object. Neither did it help that I was sure that they felt the same kind of embarrassment in front of our Western guests.

As I sat there, sinking deeper and deeper into self-pity, losing hope that I would ever become a true feminist, I heard the voice of a third sister. By now I was convinced that I knew nothing about real feminist issues, and in that way I was a bit better prepared for what was coming. As she started her speech, I took a deep breath and bent down, as if waiting for another blow to fall on my back. And it came: in a strong-sounding voice she pronounced a death sentence to all sorts of makeup! This was frightening. Certainly, I could survive without verbal abuse, perhaps even without high-heeled shoes – although I was prepared to save money for months in order to travel to Italy or Austria just to get a pair. But makeup? I thought of my mascara (that smudged a lot, so I was not supposed to cry), of my gray eyeshadow (it was not easy to get the right color; for some reason light blue and green were easier to find), my search for liquid *fond de teint*, and my lipstick that is gone in one hour. As a true feminist, after hearing her speech, I should have thrown it all in the garbage, in order to feel "wonderfully liberated," as the speaker had just suggested. Because once I had done that, I would have accepted a new "body politics." Sure, I was prepared to believe her. My problem, however, was that I had to admit to myself that not only was I unable to renounce makeup, but, perversely enough, I wanted to have much more of it – and of better quality. For a moment, I felt an urge to stand up and ask the respected speaker if her verdict included all kinds of cosmetics, like bubble-bath grains, perfumed soap, or body lotions. How many cosmetics was I allowed to use and still stay a feminist? But I did not stand up. Instead I asked myself how to cope with this conflict, that is, the desire to look good and to be a liberated woman at the same time. Why were these desires contradictory according to feminist ideology? These thoughts were on my mind as I sat there during my first feminist conference. It was treason, and I knew it.

The immediate result of this collective experience of guilt (all of us "domestic" feminists experienced it) was that we decided to raise our consciousness. Eight of us from Zagreb agreed to set up a group of our own. The idea was strengthened by the fact that the international conference in Belgrade was immediately attacked by the Communist press and dismissed as "imported bourgeois ideology." "We don't need feminism, women here are already emancipated," was the cry from the Women's Conference, the existing official organization for women. In reality, that organization was not allowed to say more than the official program of the Communist party, and bureaucratized as it was, it could not take care of women's needs at all. At any rate, the leaders of the Women's Conference were in the main the wives of the top brass of the party. Having played an important role during the Second World War, when women took part in the defense of the country, this organization had since lost its purpose entirely.

Our first coming-out as a feminist group was destined, ultimately, to be a defense against the stupid accusations launched against us. It was easy: because our critics used notorious political rhetoric and arguments (we were CIA agents!), no one could feel any sympathy for them. We were lucky that the press at that time was uncontrolled enough to publicize us, and thus a slow and painful process of building up public awareness of "women's problems" (as we called them) began.

We found a way to hold public discussions once a month, and sometimes up to 150 people would attend. Perhaps our meetings provided the only occasion at that time for women to come together and to articulate their needs. We discussed the high unemployment rate of women, violence in the family, the law on rape, or the new law on parental leave. I have to say, however, that neither high heels nor makeup was a topic on our agenda. Why? Simply because women in Yugoslavia, or in any other Communist country for that matter, did not have enough of these items. The entire notion of women's look or "image" had opposite meanings in Western and Eastern Europe.

It took me quite some time – a decade perhaps – and a lot of discussions with feminist puritans in the West to explain this paradox to them. For women living under a Communist regime, a badly made dress, ugly shoes, unattended hair, and neglected looks in general also had a political meaning, albeit a very different one. It meant that Communism as a political and economic system was not able to fulfill their basic needs. I am talking not only about freedom, food, or human rights, but also about a decent dress, sanitary napkins, toilet paper, or makeup. Every Communist regime neglected individual needs; indeed, it did not recognize individuals as such. Women dreamt about perfumes, silk blouses, or nylon stockings. They wanted to look more beautiful not because of men (or not only because of them) but in opposition to a mass society that branded this kind of aesthetics as subversive. Looking different and not submitting to uniformity makes you feel more human. On the other hand, when you can have all that your heart desires, it is easier to renounce it. It is a matter of choice: you have been using makeup, you have concluded that it contributes to your slavery as a sex object, and you consciously decide not to use it any longer. Fine – but to demand that women give up something they don't really have seems pretty repressive to me.

A couple of years later, in 1983, I attended another international feminist conference. This time it was in the United States, on Long Island. Ana, a sociologist from Poland, was the only other woman there from a Communist country. I remember that she, as well as I, wore makeup and high-heeled shoes, probably because by that time both of us had overcome our initial embarrassment about looking different from our feminist sisters in the West. But our appearance was not the only thing that bound us together. Again, we felt that we were not understood.

This time, however, we were not the only ones. A Palestinian and an Israeli feminist felt the same way. A couple of feminists from the African countries also shared our sentiments in spite of our differences. It was hard for me to listen to the problems of African or Indian women – problems that could not be compared to ours – and to discuss our problems at the same time. It was difficult to discuss what we called "formal emancipation" or emancipation on paper only: many of the women gathered looked at us with surprise, including the Americans. Didn't we have equality guaranteed by legislation? Didn't we have a year, or even two or three, of maternal leave – a thing that most women in the world could only dream of? The majority of women in the Communist world were employed and had the right to abortion, facts that seemed to speak to a genuine emancipation. Ana and I soon realized how things look from another perspective, how hard it is to convey what you think is inequality to someone from an entirely different part of the world. But what we learned and experienced for the first time was not only that there are differences between the problems facing women, depending on the country, political regime, culture, or tradition, but that we have the right to these differences, the right to voice them and to demand that they be understood by others. We also saw that one has to be careful, to examine context closely while trying to help women, because they may have priorities other than what appears obvious. Even if we all use the same vocabulary, *patriarchal society, machismo, women's rights*, etc., these words do not mean the same thing to all of us.

Yet the Long Island conference was a strange situation. The aim of the conference was to bring together feminists from all over the world (if I remember, from more than twenty countries) to discuss their experiences and see what we could learn from one another. But at the same time, it was organized and financed by the American feminists, and in those days, the early eighties, they still retained the idea of an international feminism, and of themselves as its leaders. Perhaps I am being too harsh: maybe they dominated the scene for the simple reason that they had a strong, organized mass movement, experience from many years of their own struggle, an enormous literature, world-famous women leaders, and, of course, money. On the other hand, we, a few feminists from Communist countries (not to mention those from Africa or Asia), lacked most of or all of the above. The problem was that we could not let our American sisters tell us what we had to do in our countries, and this was exactly what they wanted to do. Personally, I am ready to believe that they slipped into the role of leaders of the world feminist movement involuntarily, because I am not sure if that was what they really wanted. But I saw that their leadership caused frustration among women: how could we tell them that we could use only parts of their experience, only bits and pieces of what they so generously offered us? They were so nice, so good, so caring and willing to help, bringing us all the way from India, or Poland, or New Zealand at their expense, trying to understand our complicated political situations, spending money on us . . . and still we dared to complain that we were not understood! We did not agree with their ideas or accept their suggestions about what had to be done! We felt ungrateful, like poor relatives who ask for more than they deserve.

How could they have helped us – feminists from Yugoslavia, let alone other Communist countries? Our conditions were more difficult than anywhere else in the Western world: in Zagreb, we had to organize not as an independent group, but as a part of the Sociological Society of Croatia, as a sort of shelter. We had to be an academic, elitist group, not only because of the profile of the chief female constituents (university professors, journalists, writers, etc.) but because of our lack of access to the great majority of women who needed this kind of organization the most. In other words, opportunities for raising consciousness were very limited, and there was no possibility of organizing actions such as protests, boycotts, marches, and so on. Apart from monthly public discussions, we could publish articles in the newspapers, and so we did. But who read these newspapers? Mostly men. That was the reason for trying to start a feminist magazine in Zagreb, but we had no money for that. With this, American feminists could help us, and they promptly offered to do so. But we could not accept money from them, because we knew that it would only bring us even more trouble with the Communist authorities. The only thing we could do was to spread ideas. And the best way to get hold of these ideas was to travel abroad to conferences, to meet other women, to see what they had done, and to bring home with us the latest news and literature. It was not much, but it was essential. As a result of the not very visible but long and persistent work of a rather small group of women, many new groups popped up in Zagreb, Belgrade, and Ljubljana in the mid-eighties, which were concerned with more specific issues. For a moment it looked as if feminism had a chance to develop into a real movement in Yugoslavia. Then the war started.

In the rest of the Communist countries the situation turned out quite differently. Before 1989 it was rather difficult to pin down a single group, even an individual, who would admit to being a feminist. If you went to Czechoslovakia, you had to take a magnifying glass with you in order to find a single woman willing to, confidentially, confirm that after all, yes, she might be a feminist. "But not like those in the West," she would add, whatever that was supposed to mean. After 1989, this situation had changed, but not all that much and certainly not as quickly as the Western feminists expected. Women in Eastern Europe were very tired; they were simply worn out from decades of hard work. They wanted more money for less work and many of them simply wanted to stay home. This confused the Western feminists, who rushed into post-Communist countries hoping that with democracy winning, they could finally be of use. But they were disappointed. Are women in post-Communist countries that conservative, they asked? Don't they understand that they will be the first to lose their jobs, that they have lost their privileges and the protection they enjoyed under Communism? And that the right to abortion will be the first thing to go with the aggressive new nationalism? Yet women in the Czech and Slovak republics, in Hungary, and in Bulgaria remained rather passive. Small groups sprang up in these regions, and created a lively feminist scene, but their various activities still don't have much of an impact on society. Not even in Poland, where one would have expected a whole movement to be triggered by the winning of the anti-abortion legislation. So, what *is* going on now? Is the feeling of disappointment, sometimes expressed in the West, justified? Or is this disappointment a reflection of yet another round of our old misunderstandings? After all, what is stopping women now in post-Communist countries from articulating their needs and demanding their rights?

One has to understand that all of us lived through enormous political and economic changes, that the conditions of our existence have altered drastically, for better or worse. Capitalism is not exactly a rose garden, even if many of us believed it would be. To many people, the first task now is simply to survive, and women are no exception. On the other hand, women in Eastern Europe, throughout their lives, have been organized from "above," by the Communist party and its helping hands. When we were seven and started school, we were "pioneers" with little red scarves and uniforms. Later, we were part of the "socialist youth" organization, and then became members of the Communist party, where the women's organization was supposed to take care of our specific needs. If anything, one could say that our life was too much organized, so much so that the word *organization* became a synonym for *control*. As a result, even today we are strongly prejudiced against organizations of all kinds.

Besides, believe it or not, our women do not know how to come together and do something. They have never done it before. Their societies, with rare exceptions, had no democratic traditions. It means that they have to start from point zero, because they have no basic training in democracy. For example, they do not know what a "grassroots" group is and what it can do, what sort of power it could exercise. The spontaneous, grass-roots principle of organizing, as a basis for any kind of movement, is an unknown concept to us, and it takes time to learn it, to try it out. We simply need more time, even if we don't have it.

If I, today, had to point out one single, fundamental lesson for us – women in ex- or post-Communist countries – it would be a lesson that we learned from our contacts with Western feminists, disregarding the feminist idea itself and in spite of all small or big misunderstandings. It is precisely this: *Feminism has been, and still is, our training in democracy*. You have to identify your needs, you have to clearly articulate them, you have to set up a group yourself, you have to put pressure on institutions. In this way, you learn about your right to demand, to ask, to change, and to decide. Everyone now tends to overlook this basic principle, but every person, woman or man, who has lived in a Communist country will have to learn this principle step by step.

If only for that knowledge, I am most grateful to my feminist friends all over the Western world. They were the first to show me what democracy is all about. The second most important feature of democracy I learned is that nothing comes from "above" – not any longer. Ultimately, every person is responsible for her or his actions. This, too, I learned from feminism.

Elizabeth Renzetti

is formerly books editor for the *Globe and Mail* in Toronto and has been published in a wide variety of magazines and periodicals. She is now an arts reporter for the *Globe* and tries to behave responsibly when not interviewing rock stars.

He's My Little

K EITH RICHARDS recently told a British magazine that a blow job deserved double thanks: one for the woman who obliged, and one for the Almighty. What's not to love about this man? Seriously, now. Really. This is not a question I take lightly, for my life has been bound by two wires labeled "Keith junkie" and "woman power" that sometimes cross and threaten to fry my synapses.

Keith junkie came first in my consciousness, which gives it a kind of primacy. In the cobwebbed minutes before sleep, he told me I was the only one who could save him and asked me to sing with the Stones. He was on my record player while *The Feminine Mystique* languished on my sister's shelf, unread by me.

Even at the height of my self-absorption, consciousness still lying dormant – that is, at fourteen – I realized that Keith was a little screwed up when it came to women. I listened to "Some Girls": "Some girls get the shirt off my back and leave me with a lethal dose." This was more than a decade before feminism's progression allowed that fucking meant power, so I couldn't yet claim this as a paean to women's carnality. It just made me squirm. Even stickier was one of the next

Rock and Roll

records, as I grew more doctrinaire and he more senselessly butch: "She's my little rock 'n' roll, her tits and ass with soul, baby."

That record came out in 1981, when I was the latest in a long line of sorry misfits to enter high school – not anyone's best years, I realize, unless you truly are a freak. This was the flowering of my Keith lust, which was, I now realize, not just horniness for him, but a lust to *be* him – to be thin and ragged and cool to the point of dry ice. Instead of chubby, filled with forced and unfelt snarling and crowned with bosoms like punching bags. And bosoms a boy didn't even want to touch, I tell you, because they frightened us both.

You must understand that Keith worship is all about concavity: curving away from a thing, never straining toward it. There's no Keith fan club (or if there is, you don't want to eat lunch with them). There is no writing away for decals or newsletters. There is only the pained suffering practiced in its purest form by fourteen-year-old girls in love with spotty wankers.

I knew I wasn't alone: Patti Smith understood. And for that, I loved Patti and still wanted her head on a platter, garnished with snakes. Because she *was* Keith. Skinny, brandishing a sword emblazoned "Fuck you," and she knew guitar. She spoke the language. She was bolder, closer to commitment than a picture on the inside of a locker. She had words in a magazine, and of course she got Keith even in 1972, before Camille Paglia, before it was cool: "Keith a drunken kid," she wrote after seeing the Stones at Madison Square Garden. "He was moving so good. Thin raunchy glitter. I don't care what anyone says. He's the real Rolling Stone. He got the silver. Basic black guitar. Like a convertible. Like heartbreak hotel."

Marianne Faithfull understood, too, and I felt more comfortable with her. She seemed more fallible, more breakable than Patti, less a threat in the switchblade death derby that would ultimately be called to determine Keith's affection. She was afflicted with big tits, too, even if she didn't take the same care disguising them that I did.

The difference, though? She had him. She had him, more than once, then added pumice by saying he was the best. Marianne, some of us don't want to hear this. What we do want is the benefit of her Sacher-Masoch, Old World, Catholic schooling, which allowed her to produce insights like: "If you've read your Byron, that's Keith."

Finally, the justification I had been searching for! Once I read that, I knew I would never again have to stuff my fledgling feminist doubts back into their broken shells (a hopeless task, wouldn't you say, ladies?). I understood that Keith was a dark soul responding to a tidal pull I would never know, a purely male art-force beyond my comprehension, not just a sick sexist fuck. (And me even sicker for adoring him.)

He simply couldn't help himself; he was as much in danger of falling in love with his image — black-toothed junkie highwayman, armed with a knife in case the guitar proved impotent — as I was.

At the same time, I was developing the kind of scary persona particular to the ideologically committed post-adolescent. (I wouldn't be surprised if most of the world's death squads are made up of twenty-one-year-olds who know exactly what's wrong with the world and exactly how to fix it.) My fury rested on a shaky line of attack peppered with bullet-words like *fascist* and *patriarchy* and *oppression*. The personal was political, and I didn't let anyone get away with shit. Except Keith.

Stanley Booth, the American magazine writer, spent far too much time with the Stones in the late sixties. In his *True Adventures of the*

Rolling Stones, he followed Keith to an L.A. restaurant, where "a man and a woman passed behind him, and the woman, seeing his ragged black mane, said in a loud, drunken voice, 'You'd be cute if you put a rinse on your hair.'"

"Keith turned, smiling, showing his fangs. 'You'd be cute,' he said, 'if you put a rinse on your cunt.'"

You see my dilemma?

Then he changed, or I changed, or we both changed as we got older and our hearts grew, like the Grinch's, ten sizes plus two. Suddenly, over the course of a decade, I realized that maybe it wasn't about us versus them, that "we" didn't mean a mortal, fall-down betrayal, and Keith stopped writing about dogs and bitches.

Instead, he started to sing "Hate it when you leave" and "Eileen, won't you lean on me?" In interviews, he buzzed with the glory of his little daughters and the joys of marriage to Patti Hansen, whom he still referred to as his "old lady." All right, he wasn't completely rehabilitated but he'd taken the first painful steps. I could even be generous to *her*.

IN NOVEMBER 1995 all my planets must have been in alignment because my newspaper sent me to New York to interview Keith. "Just come back," said my editor. Not if I can help it, I thought.

What will you ask him, everyone who'd witnessed my alternating fits of drooling and uncontrollable shaking wanted to know. A little bit like asking, If you got God in a corner, what would you grill Him about? What would you have the courage to ask Him? The difference being that I didn't want to go home with God.

Then, amid the torrents of retarded advice, floated a lifesaver. "Ask him how he feels about women now," said a friend. "He's so all over the place." Ask him about women, Liz, save yourself years of therapy.

At the hotel in New York, various record company women with baffling duties floated around saying everything was "grayyyyyyyt" and talking about the bowl of potato chips as if its mere presence was a betrayal. Among the journalists was a shrink-wrapped Canadian television reporter who looked at my melted makeup and said, "You're so lucky you don't have to worry about how you look."

An exquisite Japanese radio reporter smoked calmly with me on the balcony, watching as I scribbled new questions and then discarded them as useless. I wanted to wipe some of my sweat on her. My questions seemed feeble beyond belief. I didn't care how many guitars he owns; I wanted to know how, after half a century on the earth and a quarter-century of dogged bad-ass behavior, he felt about women. This one in particular.

Outside the hotel, night was setting in, along with the paparazzi waiting for Bruce Springsteen to take a blue-collar walk downtown. Keith's internal clock operates under a set of standards not easily apparent to the sober and industrious, or even to reporters. We waited.

I picked up an interview that Keith had recently done with the British magazine *Loaded*. It was almost entirely about sex, which was not what I needed to steady my hand at that point. In it, Keith says to the interviewer, "You can have a lot more fun with a bunch of chicks than you can with a load of guys." Cha-ching! The key to plucking out the heart of his mystery!

One of the record ladies hustled me into the hallway and before I could stiffen my sinews there he was, finally, ultimately, looking just as hot as I'd always imagined. All right, looking scrawny and hammered, but it didn't make a damn bit of difference. Heathcliff, it's me, I've come home. . . .

He wandered down the hall, a tumbler of vodka and cranberry in hand, his gait suggesting a man who feels the floor tossing underfoot. One of the Stones' handlers – they are all women – had her yappy little Lhasa apso in the corridor. Keith, who once owned a short-lived dog named Syphilis, cackled as he lurched toward it, "So white 'n' fluffy you could snort it!"

The old reprobate. At fifty-one, he was still thin as an excuse, his hair a deep and suspicious brown. His face is lined but does not, contrary to accounts in the yellow press, resemble a) a cauliflower, b) a walnut, or c) a catcher's mitt.

Finally, alone in a room with an ashtray and a bed. I realized that I was staring and leaning forward as deeply as possible, a position discouraged in journalism school. I imagined a letter from the record company to my editor: "Perhaps for her own sake Ms. Renzetti should only conduct phone interviews in the future, seeing as she suffers from that unfortunate tendency to moan and salivate. . . ."

It was the most acute case of sex-related unease I've felt in an interview, a situation which is often fraught with tension – although you'd never know it from the way journalism school assiduously avoids all mention of the possibility. Perhaps it's the same in all professional training programs, but you'd think somewhere along the line somebody wise and whiskey-voiced would say: "Look, we're all professionals here, but we all like to get laid sometimes, too. There are going to be times when you're talking very seriously to somebody when all of a sudden you picture them between the sheets. It's normal. It's natural. Go back to the office and write the story, then go home and take care of yourself."

But nobody ever did say that, and the stories that get swapped are about girl reporters being chased around hotel rooms by lecherous interviewees, not vice versa. So I conducted an internal dialogue about professional ethics while trying to keep my jaw off the floor. Keith, who's as chatty as a granny at teatime, seemed oblivious. He ends every sentence with an untranslatable "Jjjmmwwhyyah," which is apparently a combination of "Do you know what I mean?" and "What a laugh."

One of the Stones' handlers came in to hurry us along and he waved her away with a limp wrist, saying, "Not now, darling" – all women are darling – "We're just getting rocking."

All righty, then. Time for the quote I'd found earlier about him preferring the company of women. "I've always felt very comfortable with the ladies," he acknowledges. "I find their talk fascinating."

Turns out that his granddad, Gus Dupree, who famously turned him on to the guitar, also taught him about sexual politics, although in postwar Britain, it was probably called Learning to Live With Them. Gus, who lived in a house with eight women, taught his jug-eared grandson the strategies of laughter, confrontation, and running like hell.

The result, forty years and a few scary spots later, is peace. "I've got a great old lady," Keith says. "And on top of that my other old ladies get along. I do get nervous sometimes when they're all in the same room together. I wonder what they're talking about."

Does he ever ask them? "No," he wheezes with his tubercular laugh. "I'm too scared."

I, on the other hand, am completely emboldened by these confessions and more than a little melted. "You know, it sounds like you're a feminist," I ask him. "What do you think?"

"I am, in a way. The best feminists are guys." Then, it's as if he realizes that he's trembling irretrievably on the brink of the nineties sensitive-guy abyss, and he turns tail and runs for the more familiar confines of the sexual battlefield. "Chicks have got to wave banners," he says. "They've always got buck teeth, look like they've never been laid in their lives, which is what they're complaining about."

I realize, with horror, that as he says this I'm still nodding away, still got that cow-eyed idiot smile on my face, still making that noise in my throat that says, "Right on, baby."

Then he brings it all back home, mumbling a conclusion that lets me know that he's a wise man, a mature man, a man worthy of a strong woman's undying devotion: "At the same time, there are certain grievances that need to be addressed."

Keith, you got me again.

Jessica Stevenson **Memoirs** of a **M**iddle-class Teenager

Jessica Stevenson

---

attends York University in Toronto.

Besides going to classes, she dances,

practises Tai Chi, reads novels, and is

a frequent zine contributor.

She published her first chapbook,

Teen Suicide (based on despair and a Goethe libretto),

when she was seventeen.

Freeing myself from the expectations that society has of me, because I am a girl is an ongoing process. I imagine that it will be something that I'll deal with for the rest of my life.

To free myself from expectations that I do not want to be part of my life, I am also going through an ongoing process of knowing myself and my own way of life. At the time that I wore makeup and put on an act around people, that became a huge part of my life, and it was so superficial. Right now I want to know and love real things- ideas, God, my spirit, my spirit in relation to the rest of the universe. I want a pure and peaceful life and I don't want superficial worries to get in the way of what is truly important in my life.

There is an idea in our society that if you act and dress a certain way, you are more female that the next person. There aren't degrees of femininity, I'm a girl and that's that. Nothing that I do could possibly render me "less female."

Being a feminist is being myself, in spite of society's claims about what girls should be.

JS.

This book is typeset in:

ATSackers

Bembo

Franklin Gothic

Snell Roundhand

CLICK

Garamond

Eurostile

ALBERTUS

Univers 49

News Gothic

Kuenstler Script

Carta

Bodoni

Trixie

Design by
Gordon Robertson